The Spiritual Journey of
Saint Patrick

Aidan J. Larkin SSC

The author gratefully thanks 'An Sagart', St Patrick's College,
Maynooth for permission to use their English translation of
Confession and the *Letter to Coroticus*.

Scripture quotations are from New Revised Standard Version
Bible, copyright © 1989 National Council of the Churches of
Christ in the United States of America. Used by permission. All
rights reserved worldwide.

ISBN 978 1 788126274

Designed by Brendan McCarthy
Typeset in Garamond Premier Pro
Printed by Johnswood Press Ltd

Messenger Publications,
37 Leeson Place, Dublin D02 E5V0
www.messenger.ie

Special thanks are offered to his Grace the
Most Reverend Eamon Martin, DD, Archbishop of Armagh,
and Primate of All Ireland.

The cover design shows St Patrick wearing the pallium. It expresses the participation of bishops, especially metropolitan archbishops, in the pastoral ministry of the pope.

This book, dedicated to the glory of God, pays homage to Daniel Conneely and Patrick Bastable, priests of the Society of Saint Columban, whose researches into the writings of St Patrick, patron of Ireland, brought to light his deep knowledge of Sacred Scripture, the Councils, and the Church Fathers.

Contents

Foreword

by Archbishop Eamon Martin

The 1950s and 1960s saw an amazing revolution in the study of St Patrick, with so much historical research that it gained a special title 'Patriciology'. The great Patrician scholar Ludwig Bieler reflects on such studies in a special edition of *Seanachas Ard Mhacha* for the Patrician Year 1961–62. In 1972 Joseph Duffy's translation of the *Confession* into English and his comments helped to renew the interest of the general public and further open up the study of Patrick's background, life and mission to a new generation.

Fr Aidan J. Larkin adds to our interest in this book *The Spiritual Journey of St Patrick*. He reflects on the background of Patrick not only by absorbing the modern research on Patrick but also by offering his own fresh comments, particularly on Patrick's spirituality, his use of Scripture, and emphasising the traces and resonances of the writings of the Fathers on Patrick's Letters.

The research work that has inspired Fr Larkin is primarily that of Fr Daniel Conneely (Society of St Columban), much of which is published posthumously in the book *The Letters of Saint Patrick* edited and presented by Patrick Bastable together with Thomas Finan, Maurice Hogan, Thomas Norris and Padraig O Fiannachta of St Patrick's College, Maynooth (An Sagart, 1993). Fr Larkin responds to Fr Daniel Conneely's desire that the main ideas of his research on St Patrick should be made available in simplified form for the general reader. Faithful to Fr Conneely's text, Fr Larkin shows that the true value of both the *Confession* and the *Letter to Coroticus* lies in the accounts of Patrick's inner life and spiritual journey which they gave us.

Fr Larkin proceeds to give an account of St Patrick's religious experience first as a youth and slave boy, later as a priest and bishop. Fr Larkin then reflects on St Patrick's inner quest, which he maintained even during his hours of darkness. Finally, he has tried to put before the reader Patrick's own spiritual insights as bishop and pastor that link him with the Fathers of the Church, particularly with St Augustine.

Fr Conneely's work constitutes a paradigm shift in Patrician studies. Much previous scholarly research tended to concentrate mainly on historical matters, for example, the value of Patrick's correspondence for biographical information, the dates of his missionary career in Ireland, the quality of his Latin unfavourably compared with classical Latin. Not enough attention perhaps had been given to the rich spiritual and theological content contained therein. Fr Conneely recognised and demonstrated that Patrick, whose familiarity with the Bible was already well known, was also well versed in the theology of the Fathers of the Church.

It is suggested that the *Confession*, being of a confessional-autobiographical genre, should be read primarily as an account of Patrick's religious experience, his inner spiritual journey. It began with his search for God during his years of captivity, his subsequent encounter with God, the joys and sorrows of his missionary experience among the pagan Irish, and the deepening of his spiritual life as he reached old age when he penned his *Confession*.

The reader of Fr Larkin's book will therefore gain personally a great insight into Patrick's spirituality. Perhaps this will help all of us, laity and clergy alike, to avoid the temptation towards a token patriotic celebration of the Feast of St Patrick. Speaking of his generation Patrick says, 'We distanced ourselves from God and did not observe his commandments.' Fr Larkin shows us how we can all benefit from a careful reflection on the life and writings of Patrick, pointing out how Patrick's theology resonates with the teaching of St Augustine, the Doctor of Grace.

Patrick's reason for writing was, in the first place, to give thanks to God who had never deserted him during his journey through life. He also wanted to give witness to what God had done in his life to stir up in his readers a religious search that would bring about their conversion and return to God, because God is a loving God, rich in mercy.

Patrick's writings are therefore particularly relevant in the pontificate of Francis that highlights mercy as God's unmerited love for wayward human beings unforgettably portrayed in the parable of the Merciful Father (Lk 15:11–32). They help us recognise who God really is and who we are. For Jesus reveals the true nature of God as that of a Father who never gives up until he has forgiven his wandering children with compassion and mercy when they return to him. Patrick's religious experience as portrayed in his correspondence is an eloquent confirmation of that truth.

We might recall words written by St Augustine, 'Ours is the religion which constitutes the universal way of liberation for the soul, for no soul can be set free except by it. It is the Royal road which alone leads to the Kingdom whose greatness does not sway with the vicissitudes of time but stands immovable on the solid ground of eternity ... This is the way which belongs, not to one nation only, but to all ... for the Mediator Himself said ... that penance and the remission of sins would be preached in His name to all the nations' (*De Civitate Dei,* X, 32).

In this era of 'new evangelisation' we find in Patrick's writings inspiration to see our faith as life in Christ. We are indeed indebted to Fr Larkin for making available Patrick's spiritual journey in a very readable manner, and that may be summed up in the words of the Psalm: 'What return can I make to the Lord for his goodness to me' (116:12).

† *Eamon Martin*
Archbishop of Armagh

Preface

Many legends, stories and traditions have grown up over the centuries regarding Ireland's most famous saint. It is necessary, therefore, to separate the man from the myth by returning to St Patrick's own writings, namely, the *Letter to Coroticus* and what has become known as his *Confession*. Today, it is generally accepted that both were penned by Patrick himself. Despite these, very little by way of precise dates and places is known about him. Neither document attempts to give a history of his life; both are reactions to crises in his life.

The first is a stern letter to Coroticus, a British slave owner who had massacred and enslaved Irish Christians. Patrick asserts his authority as bishop and is outraged at the treatment of his newly baptised Christians. What also emerges from this letter is Patrick's great love for the Irish. This was first enkindled when he heard their call to come and walk among them once more. But above all, his love is shown in the way he dedicated his life to their welfare and eternal salvation.

The so-called *Confession* was written towards the end of his life as he struggled to understand God's life-plan for him. What he wanted to highlight was God's goodness and mercy and his amazing grace evident in the success of his mission to the Irish. In a simple written account, Patrick's trust in God and his gratitude towards him who had achieved so much through such a weak instrument, shine out. This in no way detracts from the unique light his *Confession* casts on this humble missionary of Christ who brought his Gospel of love to the Irish people. A great missionary looked back on his life and saw the labyrinthine pattern of God's wonderful design.

As he reviews his life journey, which he admits was full of faults and shortcomings, and in the apparently haphazard events of his life, so inexplicable when they occurred, he now sees the hand of God at work in which his hidden plan for the salvation of the Irish is realised. No extraordinary wonders marked his progress throughout Ireland, nevertheless, he touched the hearts of young people who flocked to him and committed their lives to following Christ in the priesthood and religious life.

The essential knowledge about a saint lies not so much in dates and places, but rather in his holiness, his values, what inspired him and his spiritual wrestlings. On these points we are well informed. Patrick sets the record straight regarding his mission and underscores the role God had in it. Often misunderstood in the past, Patrick hoped that his readers would finally grasp how he regarded his long, arduous but ultimately successful mission. His story is one of God's grace that leads to wonder and thanksgiving.

Fr Aidan Larkin has responded magnificently to the desire of Fr Daniel Conneely that his research on St Patrick would be made available to the general reader. He accomplishes this by highlighting the inner life and spiritual journey of St Patrick, as well as his spiritual doctrine that links him to the Fathers of the Church. Fr Larkin traces the crucial events of Patrick's religious experience that began with his search for God during his captivity until he reached old age when he composed his *Confession*. His presentation of Patrick's spiritual journey may serve to stir up in readers a similar religious search that would bring about their return to God or deepen their relationship with him. The author sees Patrick's religious experience as a confirmation of the truth that God is love and rich in mercy, something Pope Francis never tires of reminding us. We are indebted to Fr Larkin for a very engaging and engrossing account of Patrick's spiritual journey.

Fr Maurice Hogan SSC

Introduction

Among the many treasures of Trinity College, Dublin, the *Book of Kells*, an illuminated manuscript of the four Gospels, has pride of place. Not only is it the supreme achievement of medieval Irish monastic art, but it also bears powerful witness to the profound reverence in which the early Irish Church held the Sacred Scriptures.

Reverence and love are taught chiefly by example. We may then well ask: who was it that, by his example, taught the Irish to love and reverence the Word of God so deeply? It was St Patrick, surely, a man whose heart and mind were nourished by constant reading of the Sacred Scriptures.

Scholars tell us that in the *Confession* and the *Letter to Coroticus*, the only two documents written by Patrick, he alludes to no less than fifty-four books of the Bible. In first place are the Psalms, then Paul's Letter to the Romans, the Acts of the Apostles, the Gospel according to Matthew, and finally, the First and Second Letters of St Paul to the Corinthians. It comes as a surprise to many people, however, to learn that not only was Patrick extremely well read in Sacred Scripture, he also had a wide knowledge of the writings of the Latin Fathers. The Latin Fathers, also known as the Church Fathers, were a group of theologians who established the intellectual and doctrinal foundations of Christianity. They flourished during the fourth and fifth century and included Cyprian, Jerome and Augustine. The first to conduct an extended study of the influence of the Fathers on Patrick was Fr Daniel Conneely (1911–1986). Ludwig Bieler and George Misch had noted connections between Patrick and Cyprian, Jerome, Anthony and Augustine.[1] During the Patrician Year of 1961, while Conneely was engaged in making a new translation of Patrick's writings, his attention was drawn to the many quotations from and allusions to the Latin Fa

---

1   Ludwig Bieler, 'The Place of Saint Patrick in Latin Language and Literature', *Vigiliae Christianae*, vol. 6, no. 2 (Apr., 1952), pp. 65–98; George Misch, *Geschicte der Autobiographie*, Leipzig, 1907.

thers previously passed over without scrutiny by him and other scholars.[2] He began to take copious notes. His note taking led him to the realisation that the writings of Patrick showed that he was well read in the early general councils of the Church and the Latin Fathers, notably Augustine. He also believed that earlier scholars had overlooked the theological import of the Patrick's writings, in particular, the themes of mission and salvation, and then the contribution of the Church Fathers. We are all in Conneely's debt, for he has given us a new insight into the mind and heart of Patrick and changed forever the way in which we approach his writings.

Christianity was brought to Ireland in the fifth century AD. Along with the Gospel message came the Latin language and the Roman script. The oldest Latin texts that have come down to us in Ireland are the *Confession* and the *Letter to Coroticus*. A collection of documents called the *Book of Armagh*, kept in the library of Trinity College, Dublin, includes an incomplete manuscript of the *Confession*. It is usually dated to the beginning of the ninth century. The scribe was a certain Ferdomnach. Complete manuscripts of the *Letter to Coroticus* and the *Confession* are kept in the Bibliothèque Nationale de France in Paris, in the British Library in London, and in other libraries in Britain and France.

During the nineteenth century and well into the twentieth, most students of early Irish history tended to consider the *Confession* and the *Letter to Coroticus* mainly as sources they could draw on in order to write the history of early Irish society and construct an orderly narrative of the life and mission of Patrick. It gradually became clear that neither the *Letter to Coroticus* nor the *Confession* could yield sufficient historical data of the kind historians needed. As a result, many questions, including those about Patrick's place and date of birth, have remained unanswered up to the present.

As the twentieth century advanced, some students began to find it more rewarding to read the *Confession* as a revelation of Patrick's inner

2   See D. A. Binchy in 'Patrick and his Biographers, Ancient and Modern', Part II, 'Historical Value of the Sources', p. 38, in *Studia Hibernica*, no. 2, 1962, p. 56, 'These (the writings of Patrick) were never intended to provide information for historians.'

spiritual journey: his search for God, his encounter with God, his joys and his sorrows. The realisation dawned that the *Confession* was not an example of historiography. It belonged to a different literary genre, what scholars have called 'confessional-autobiographical'; a genre requiring a distinct manner of reading and interpretation. The move away from debates about dates and places caused a renewal of interest in what the *Confession* and the *Letter to Coroticus* actually say and encouraged research into the history of the development of the confessional genre. Patriciology set off in a direction that has opened up new perspectives and made the *Confession* and *Letter to Coroticus* accessible to the non-academic reader.

After the death of Conneely, the Rev. Dr Patrick Bastable (1918–1992), a lecturer in philosophy in University College Dublin (UCD), and Rev. Dr Maurice Hogan, Prof. of Sacred Scripture at St Patrick's College Maynooth, both priests of the Society of St Columban, together with Prof. Teresa Iglesias, of UCD, took charge of Conneely's notebooks and prepared them for publication. The work which finally resulted, entitled *The Letters of Saint Patrick,* was published by An Sagart at Maynooth in 1993. In his preface, Fr Bastable stated that, 'Fr Conneely's work had a distinct and definite goal: to consider whether on the basis of textual enquiry one could observe *a clear link between the writings of St Patrick and those of the Fathers. The result of his research puts such linkage beyond any reasonable doubt.*'[3] Furthermore, Conneely had hoped not only to communicate his research to scholars but also his new translation of the two texts with a commentary on their theological, missiological and spiritual content. People could then see in the text, substantially, what was there to be seen in the fifth century. In the person of Patrick, they would be given an experience of a Churchman of great competence, typically patristic in many qualities of his thought and presentation. Sadly, death prevented both Conneely and Bastable from fulfilling this project.

In the summer of 2012, Rev. Dr Maurice Hogan invited me to write something about the theological, missiological and spiritual content of the two documents, along the lines which Conneely would have

3   Italics are Bastable's.

17

wished.

For practical reasons, I decided to limit my discussion to three of the best known Latin Fathers: Augustine, bishop of Hippo in north Africa, Hilary of Poitiers, theologian and apologist, and Cyprian of Carthage, bishop and martyr.

Patrick is often difficult to read, and his meaning is often hard to grasp. My purpose in this book is not to resolve every problem Patrick's writings pose. Instead, my aim is pastoral. I wish to evangelise. I wish to put myself at the service of God, and of Patrick, who in heaven prays continuously for his people here on earth.

Aidan J. Larkin SSC

Part 1:
Patrick: His Life And Work

1: The Historical Patrick and Popular Tradition

'Nothing in the Irish annals, or in any other Irish source, can be proved to be genuine reminiscence of Patrick or his activities; we are forced to rely on his *Confession* and *Letter* for the saint's own words.' [4]

The truth is that few people approach Patrick through his writings. Instead they come to know him through the popular religious traditions of the Irish people. We absorbed the stories we heard about him at home from our parents, in school from our teachers, and in church from our priests. Some things we learned were legends, often very beautiful, as for example the legend of Patrick and the fawn. We also learned songs and hymns like 'Hail, Glorious St Patrick', or, 'Dóchas linn, Naomh Pádraig'. We came to know the Christian meaning of the shamrock, which Patrick is said to have used to teach the mystery of the Blessed Trinity. We wore the shamrock on St Patrick's Day. We 'remember' the banishment of the snakes from Ireland by Patrick. Even jokes and ballads have influenced our ways of thinking about Patrick, for example, 'Saint Patrick was a gentleman'. We have statues of Patrick, such as on the Hill of Tara or on the Hill of Slemish.

Part of what contributes to the popular image of Patrick comes from written sources such as the works of seventh-century writers like Muirchú and Tirechán,[5] and the compiler of the late ninth-century *Vita Tripartita*. These works, contained in the *Book of Armagh*, are not generally considered 'historical' as we understand the term today. Muirchú in particular conveys a vivid image of Patrick, a saint mighty

4   Daibhi Ó Cróinín, *Early Medieval Ireland: 400–1200*, Abingdon: Routledge, 1995, p. 23.
5   See Bieler (ed.), *The Patrician Texts in the Book of Armagh*, Dublin: DIAS, 1952.

21

in word and deed, like Moses or Elijah, able to confront kings like the pharaoh of Egypt or the high king of Ireland, with their magicians and powerful men, but Muirchú's work is not historical, in the proper meaning of the term.

Popular tradition can be a vehicle for the transmission of faith in the God whom Christ revealed and Patrick preached. It is not therefore automatically to be disregarded or dismissed. Still, for all that, though I will make occasional references to Muirchú and Tírechán, the focus will be on what we can discover by a careful reading of what Patrick himself wrote. This book then looks at Patrick through the lens of the *Confession (C)* and the *Letter to Coroticus (LC)*.

Ireland before Patrick

It is widely believed that there were communities of Christians already in existence in Ireland before the arrival of Patrick. During the fifth century there was much trade between Ireland and the Roman provinces of Britain and Gaul, including trade in slaves. As well as ordinary merchandise, some British merchants probably brought the Christian faith with them. There were also refugees in Ireland from Gaul and Britain as the Roman government of these provinces gradually collapsed. Some may have been Christians and may have evangelised the people they encountered in Ireland.

Indeed there is linguistic evidence that Christianity arrived in Ireland as early as the first half of the fourth century.[6] Michael Richter believes that there is 'a not inconsiderable corpus of early Latin loan words' in the Irish language, which is evidence of the existence of an organised Christian community in the fourth century.

The *Chronicle* of Prosper of Aquitaine records that in the year 431 Pope Celestine, motivated by concern lest Pelagianism should become established in Ireland, ordained a certain Palladius 'as first bishop, for the Irish believing in Christ'.[7] It is believed he preached in Ireland although he was soon banished by the King of Leinster.

6   Michael Richter, *Medieval Ireland,* Dublin: Gill and Macmillan, 2005, pp. 45–6.
7   See J. Kenney, *The Sources for the Early History of Ireland: Ecclesiastical – An Introduction and Guide,* Dublin: Four Courts Press, 1993.

Pelagianism was a fifth-century heresy taught by Pelagius (c. 354–c. 418), who was believed to be of Celtic-British origin. According to Pelagianism human beings have the free will to choose between good and evil and can be wholly good. Pelagius's disciple Celestius denied the doctrine of original sin.[8] Pelagius and Augustine (354–430) were the central figures in the Pelagian controversy. Augustine argued against Pelagius that human beings depend on the grace of God. Pelagianism was condemned at the Second Council of Ephesus (431).

Pelagianism was not the only major heresy in Patrick's time. Arianism maintains that the Son (Christ) was created by God and is not self-existent and immutable like God. Arianism arose from the teachings of Arius (c. 250–336). Arianism was opposed by the Church Fathers. There are both anti-Pelagian and anti-Arian strands in the writings of Patrick.

The stages of Patrick's life

There were three major stages or turning points of Patrick's life, each of which was marked by a great personal crisis.

The first stage began when, at the age of sixteen, his boyhood was brought to an abrupt and brutal end at the hands of kidnappers, who captured him and sold him into slavery 'along with many thousand others' (*C*, 1).[8.1] This stage lasted for six years. Patrick, responding to the divine call, finally escaped and made his way home. He was the first Roman citizen that we know of to ever succeed in escaping from captivity and live to tell the tale.

The second stage followed his decision to respond to the call of God and return to Ireland as a missionary. It included his ordination first as a priest and later as a bishop. During this time one of his fledging communities suffered an attack by Pictish pirates. Many men were put to the sword and many women carried off into slavery, and worse. This atrocity occasioned the *Letter to Coroticus*, which also included an extended defence of Patrick's episcopal authority. We are reminded of the Second Letter of Paul to the Corinthians, written by him in order to defend his episcopal authority in the face of a rebellious community.

8   'Pelagius', *Britannica* (website), https://www.britannica.com/biography/Pelagius-Christian-theologian.

23

Finally, we come to the third stage, which included the revelation of the sins of his boyhood, his trial by a tribunal of his seniors, his conviction, and, finally, removal from office. Patrick would not have been human if he had not been shaken to the core by these events.

The first stage: enslavement and escape

We do not know the exact year of Patrick's birth, but a date some time during the last decade of the fourth century or the first decade of the fifth is a reasonable guess.[9] Patrick was born into a Romano-British family in the Roman province of Britain in the last years of its existence, the son of a government official who was also a deacon in the Church. His father's name was Calpornius. Surprisingly, Patrick does not mention his mother, though he does refer to his grandfather, Potitus, who was a priest. We do not know whether he had brothers and sisters. The village where his family lived was named *Bannavem Taburniae*. It may have been somewhere on the west coast of Britain, maybe in the vicinity of Bristol, or more to the north, near Carlisle.[10]

Calpornius held the office of *decurio,* a lifelong (and in the late empire hereditary) appointment which made him*, ex officio*, a member of the municipal senate.[11] The family certainly belonged to the provincial gentry, most of whom, we may assume, were Christians. Because of his father's office as a *decurio* the family was categorised as 'upper class'. Patrick was born of good family. Because his grandfather was a priest and his father a deacon, Patrick was probably looked upon as belonging to an 'ecclesiastical' family. In the *Letter to Coroticus* he refers to his social position, 'I am a free man', he says, 'I am the son of a *decurio*. The

9   Joseph Duffy argues for the years 462 for the commencement Patrick's mission and 491-3 for his death These dates are now widely accepted. See, Duffy, *Patrick in His Own Words*, Dublin: Veritas, 2000.

10   Marcus Losack put forward a new theory of Patrick's origins which locates his place of birth in post-Roman Gaul. However, Pádraig McCarthy, an expert on Patrick at the Royal Irish Academy, writing in the letters page of *The Irish Times*, 19 November 2013, comments, 'There are various theories about the whereabouts of *Bannavem Taburniae*; none is conclusive. I do not give unqualified support for any one theory. We simply do not have enough information to be sure of Patrick's place of origin, whether Brittany, as Rev. Losack argues, or Britain, as others hold. Either is possible.' For Losack's theory see, *Rediscovering St Patrick: A New Theory of Origins*, Dublin: Columba Press, 2013.

11   In the late empire the class of *decuriones* became hereditary. If Patrick's life had followed a normal course he would eventually have succeeded his father in an important role in society.

fact is that for the benefit of others I sold my freeborn state[12] – I am not ashamed of it, and I have no regrets' (*LC*, 9).

The family were slave owners. This was normal for a family of Patrick's background. It is reasonable to suppose that Patrick lived in a comfortable town house with domestic slaves to wait upon him. We know that his father also possessed a 'modest country estate' (*C*, 1), which would have included a dwelling as its centrepiece. Patrick probably spoke archaic Welsh with the household slaves. Latin was therefore not his only language, perhaps not even the dominant one. Christine Mohrmann suggests that he was bilingual.[13] At the time of his capture he was just sixteen. He would already have received the *toga virilis*, the Roman garment of manhood, which was given to a boy when he reached fourteen, though he still refers to himself as a boy, 'As an adolescent, indeed almost as a speechless boy, I was taken captive before I knew what I should seek and what I should avoid ' (*C*, 10).

Patrick's father, because he was a *decurio*, was also a life member of the municipal senate. *Decuriones* wore a toga with a purple stripe. Qualifications for appointment included wealth, age, free birth, and reputation. They were selected mainly from among those who were or had been magistrates. Patrick's father therefore had probably been a magistrate earlier in his career. *Decuriones* ran local government (including external relations) in both colonies and municipalities. They exercised important supervisory functions on behalf of the Imperial authorities in regard to the collection of taxes. They were on this account alone indispensable to the running of the Empire. The office they held brought other privileges. For example, if a *decurio* should commit an offence he would receive a much milder punishment. Thus they were generally exempt from the death penalty.

Some historians have speculated that Patrick's father was not a man dedicated to his sacred office as a deacon[14] and that he may even have acquired the diaconate because it rendered him immune from financial

---

12 R. P. C. Hanson translates '*nobilitas*' as 'aristocratic status'. I see in this an incipient *kenosis* theology (i.e. theology of self-emptying).

13 Christine Mohrmann, *The Latin of Saint Patrick: Four Lectures*, Dublin Institute for Advanced Studies, 2009, pp. 9, 45.

14 See R. C. P. Hanson, *The Life and Writings of the Historical Saint Patrick*, New York: Seabury Press, 1983, pp. 67, 77.

sanctions possibly arising from unsatisfactory fulfilment of the duties which pertained to his office as an overseer of the imperial revenue.[15]

In virtue of his father's roles as a deacon and a *decurio,* Patrick too possessed high social status. It would be an over-statement to describe Patrick as a rich young man, but he certainly grew up as a member of a family whose father was a leading citizen. But, before long, his status and privileges would be swept away, as the Roman legions, whose mission was to defend the province of Britain, were withdrawn, never to be replaced. In due course Patrick might have inherited his father's job and status, but, as we shall see, God would lead him along a very different path, and Patrick would adhere to the divine plan, which he describes as 'the Gift of God' (*C,* 14, 33, 62). It was indeed the gift of God, but paradoxically, at the same time, a gift 'costing not less than everything'.[16] Patrick would empty himself in imitation of Christ as is described in Philippians, '[Christ] emptied himself, taking the form of a slave' (Phil 2:7). He would pay the price and think nothing of it because he did it out of love.

As a boy belonging to the upper class, Patrick was educated in the Roman fashion. He received the first two 'stages' of a Roman education, an elementary education focused on reading and writing (ages 7–11) and a secondary education focused on the correct use of Latin (ages 12–16). This secondary education included Latin composition and the reading of some of the easier passages of authors like Cicero and Virgil. As a Christian, Patrick would also have read Sacred Scripture, especially the Psalms. The third 'stage' of Roman education focused on rhetoric (the skills necessary for effective public speaking and acquaintance with Greek philosophy and Roman law). Patrick never got to this third stage, because of his capture by slave traders.

David Howlett has shown that as a mature man Patrick was not skilled in writing in the elegant prose of classical Latin.[17] Rather, he wrote in a style of Latin that imitated biblical and patristic Latin, employing a 'chiastic' structure typical of Hebrew poetry and prose (see

---

15 Walsh and Bradley, *A History of the Irish Church 400–700 AD,* Dublin: Columba Press, 1991, p. 24.
16 See Dietrich Bonhoeffer, *The Cost of Discipleship,* Touchstone, 1995.
17 David Howlett, *The Book of Letters of St Patrick the Bishop,* Dublin: Four Courts Press, 1994.

page 54). In the style of the *Confession* and *Letter to Coroticus*, we can see the influence on Patrick of both the disruption to his intended education and his own study of the Bible and the Church Fathers.

Throughout his life Patrick remained sensitive about his interrupted education. He introduced himself in the *Confession* as *peccator*, 'a sinner' and, coming a close second, he applied to himself the word *'rusticissimus'*, meaning 'very uncultured and unlettered'.[18] He is not thinking of general social skills but more narrowly of skill with language (Latin). He compared himself unfavourably with those who have received the benefits of a full classical education, 'I have had to change my language and speak that of a foreign people as may be easily proved from the flavour of my writing which shows how poorly I am instructed and how little skilled in expressing myself' (*C*, 9). All this led him to hesitate before putting pen to paper. A little earlier he said, 'I had long ago thought of writing but had hesitated until now for fear of what critics would say' (*C*, 9).[19] He was very human: he didn't want to be laughed at for the quality of his Latin, though he was a man with a natural gift of self-expression.

When Patrick was just sixteen he was seized by pirates or slave traders and taken to Ireland along with 'so many thousands of people' (*C*, 1). He was humbled dramatically and brutally. He says that this happened to him and his companions 'in accordance with our deserts' (*C*, 1).[20] The conviction that continued sinfulness and refusal to repent are a path that leads to disaster – even in this life – is deeply biblical. The Psalmist says, 'for the Lord watches over the way of the righteous, but the way of the wicked will perish' (Ps 1:6). Paul says, 'the wages of sin

18 *'Rusticitas'* means principally the lack of proficiency in literary Latin. The ability to write polished Latin was expected of a bishop in post-Roman Gaul. Bishops in Gaul usually came from aristocratic families. Many were the sons of former imperial officials. They were well versed in Classical letters and culture. To them, among others, Patrick may have ironically applied the term *'dominicati rhetorici'* (*C*, 13). For a discussion of this term, see Mohrmann, *Four Lectures*, p. 30.

19 Elizabeth McLuhan characterises Patrick differently, 'Patrick is no bumbling rube apologising for his lack of learning. Rather, he wears his lack of human teaching as a badge of honour with the knowledge that his mission and his understanding come directly from God.' See McLuhan, 'The Metaphor and Reality of Slavery' in Carey, Herbert, O Riain (eds), *Saints and Scholars: Studies in Irish Hagiography*, Dublin: Four Courts Press, 2001, p. 63.

20 Duffy translates, 'We deserved this fate'. Walsh and Bradley, *A History of the Irish Church*, p. 24.

is death' (Rom 6:23). In the Bible, the downfall first of the kingdom of Israel and then Judah were attributed to the anger of God on account of man's sin (Jer 31:10). Faced with sin and a stubborn refusal to repent, God humbled his people, scattering his flock and allowing them to be exiled and enslaved by their enemies. We can see this clearly in the Book of Ezekiel: 'when the house of Israel lived on their own soil, they defiled it with their ways and their deeds … So I poured out my wrath upon them … I scattered them among the nations … in accordance with their conduct and their deeds I judged them. But when they came to the nations, wherever they came, they profaned my holy name, in that it was said of them, "These are the people of the Lord, yet they had to go out of his land"' (Ezek 36:16–21).

But God never abandoned his people completely. He always left a remnant from which new life could spring. We read in Isaiah 11:1, 'A shoot shall come out from the stump of Jesse'. In Jeremiah 23:3, 'Then I myself will gather the remnant of my flock out of all the lands where I have driven them, and I will bring them back to their fold'. This is what happened in Patrick's case too, though at a personal, individual level. God allowed Patrick's life to be shattered, but he did so in order that Patrick might receive new life, might be re-born of God.

The drudgery of the life of a slave-boy was not the totality of Patrick's experience during his time in Ireland. During the six years he spent 'herding flocks … in the woods and on the mountain' (*C*, 16), exposed to the elements night and day, he turned to God with all his heart and soul. God was with him. 'God watched over me before I knew him' (*C*, 2), he says. 'I earnestly sought him, and there I found him' (*C*, 33) . The frightened youth became a man of profound prayer. He learned to know God and experienced his fatherly care and protection, 'God kept me safe and comforted me as a father would his son' (*C*, 2). He was graced with the intimate consolations of the Holy Spirit and filled with love of Christ who, as he tells us, helped him, especially when, on one occasion, he was harassed by Satan. 'I believe that I was aided by Christ my Lord, and that His Spirit was even then crying out on my behalf' (*C*, 20).

In the Bible, visions, dreams, and voices are relatively common.[21] They are a means of communicating the Divine Will to the recipient. Patrick tells us that one night while he was fasting, in his sleep, he heard a voice saying to him, 'Look, your ship is ready' (*C*, 17). The ship was at a distance of perhaps two hundred miles. But Patrick, undaunted, took to flight, leaving his master with whom he had been for six years. '[I] journeyed by the power of God, who directed my way unto my good, and I feared nothing until I reached that ship' (*C*, 17). After an initial rejection by the ship's captain he was finally allowed to go aboard. After three days they reached land, and for twenty-eight days they travelled through barren land, *per desertum*,[22] suffering hunger until Patrick, at the insistence of the captain and crew, prayed for the whole ship's company and food appeared in the shape of a herd of pigs, some of which they slaughtered and ate. Finally, they reached their destination, which most probably was Britain. Here Patrick evokes the desert trials of Jesus (Mt 4:2) and the Israelites (Ex 15–17).

For many people, this story of Patrick's enslavement evokes the first part of the biblical story of Joseph (Gen 37). Others discern in it a resonance of the narrative of Augustine's departure for Rome in the *Confessions*,[23] raising the general question of possible literary dependence of Patrick on Augustine. Now that Patrick was back in Britain, his family, having recovered him, 'after all the many troubles he had endured', naturally did not wish to lose him again (*C*, 23). But lose him they would. Their loss would be Ireland's gain. We know of no Roman citizen captured by raiders before Patrick who had ever lived to tell the tale, but by the grace of God, who reached out to him in mercy and love, Patrick lived to accept and fulfil the sacred mission God had reserved for him.

---

21 See Peter Dronke, 'St Patrick's Reading', *CMCS* 1 (Summer, 1981), pp. 21–38. For more detail see Conneely, *The Letters of Saint Patrick,* Chapter Two, 'Literary genre of Patrick's pastoral letters (b)', written by Thomas Finan. Patrick speaks frequently of 'visions of the night' (*C*, 20, 21, 23, 24, 29). See also, W. Swan, 'The Experience of God in the writings of St Patrick, reworking a faith received', a doctoral thesis presented in the Gregorian University, Rome, 2012

22 Meaning 'through the desert'.

23 Augustine, *Confessions*, Book V, 88.

The second stage: Patrick's vocation

'I saw in a vision of the night ... a man coming ... with countless letters' (*C*, 23).[24] These letters are 'the voice of the Irish' (*C*, 23), *glór na nGael*. Described by Patrick as 'a vision of the night', the passage is also a vocation story, reminiscent of the passage in Acts where Paul in a vision is called to go to Macedonia (Acts 16:9), or the call of the youthful Samuel as he slept in the sanctuary in Shiloh (1 Sam 3). The vision of the night takes place after Patrick had escaped from captivity in Ireland and returned to his home in Britain. By means of it, God calls Patrick, entrusting to him the mission of making God known to this people who belong to God but have no knowledge of the Gospel.[25]

At the burning bush, God tells Moses that he has witnessed the oppression of his people and has come down to rescue them (Ex 3). Moses must lead them out of Egypt. God's plan is to make a Covenant with them, to make them his own chosen people. So also in the case of the Irish; Patrick is set free from captivity in order that he may fulfil the mission God gives him of emancipating the Irish from the darkness of those who have no knowledge of the Gospel. To them the words of Isaiah will apply, 'The people that walked in darkness have seen a great light' (Isa 9:1). God will lead them into a new life as 'a people of the Lord'.

'I was greatly troubled' (*C*, 23), Patrick says, yet he answers God's call by offering his whole life in service from that moment on. We think of Our Lady's consent, at the Annunciation, 'Here am I, the servant of the Lord; let it be with me according to your word' (Lk 1:38), and, supremely, that of Christ himself, 'Here I am, Lord, I come to do your will' (Hb 10:7). His response means that the cry of the Irish is heard in heaven. Writing his *Confession* as he approaches the end of his life, Patrick can now see that God's plan has been fulfilled and his heart is filled with immense gratitude. 'Thanks be to God that after many years He granted them according to their cry' (*C*, 23).

24 Patrick describes himself as a 'letter of Christ' (*C*, 11) quoting 2 Cor 3:2, 'the best letter of recommendation'.

25 *Confession* 23 includes a reference to the wood of Vocluth. This place has never been securely identified. It was probably in the west, in County Mayo. For an interesting attempt at a different solution see J. McErlean, 'Silva Focluti', in the *Revue Bollandiste*.

We possess no factual information about this period of Patrick's life. Some British scholars, notably Kenneth Jackson, arguing from a study of Patrick's Latin, hold that he studied in Britain and had little knowledge of continental Europe.[26] On the other hand, Patrick refers to his brethren in Gaul, 'I would most dearly love to make that journey, so as to see my homeland and family; not only that, but also [to proceed] as far as Gaul to visit the brethren [fellow students?] and see the face of the saints of my Lord' (*C*, 43). This suggests familiarity with Gaul where he has friends.[27] Bieler believes that he studied under Germanus in Auxerre – Germanus visited Britain twice to preach against the Pelagian heresy. It is not impossible that Patrick may have met him. Muirchú says that Patrick spent a considerable period of time at Auxerre, but critics argue that Muirchú wanted to construct a pedigree for Patrick and for this reason linked him to the great Germanus. Others, among them John Ryan SJ, believe that he studied in the monastery of Lérins, situated off the southern coast of Gaul, near Nice. The monastery was founded in 410 by Honoratus of Arles and became a flourishing centre of monastic life and theological study. It has been called 'an academy for bishops'. If we are right in believing that Patrick studied for a time on Lérins, then we are probably also right in believing that his teachers were monks. His sympathy with monasticism is very obvious. If this view is correct, we can say that the father of Irish Christianity was a man who understood and sympathised with the monastic ideal, even if he was not himself a monk. This would account for his high esteem for consecrated celibacy and his personal commitment to it (*C*, 44).

Duffy says that in recent years Latin scholars have been coming round to the view that the intellectual milieu of a place like Lérins is not at all incompatible with the hitherto unsuspected sophisticated and subtle overtones of Patrick's writings. None of these arguments of course prove that Patrick studied at Lérins. What they indicate is that he is more likely to have received his clerical formation in Gaul than

26 See Kenneth Jackson, *Language and History in Early Britain,* Dublin: Four Courts Press, 2000.
27 Muirchú's *Life* says that Patrick remained in Gaul a long time.

in Britain.[28]

It is probable that during these years Patrick was initiated into the writings of the Latin Fathers. This, if correct, was an important milestone in his religious development. As we will see, Patrick's personal religious culture, in addition to his daily practice of *lectio divina*,[29] was deeply formed by his contact with the writings of the Fathers.

When did Patrick's mission to Ireland begin and when did it end? If the date 431, given for Palladius, is correct, then Patrick could not have begun his mission earlier than 432. The years 432–461 for the beginning of Patrick's activity in Ireland until his death had been widely accepted since the beginning of the twentieth century, principally on the authority of the distinguished Trinity College historian, J. B. Bury.[30] Scholars have shown that the Patrician entries in the so-called fifth century Annals (on which the 'two Patricks' theory primarily relies for its case) lack validity.[31] Duffy tells us that the weight of scholarly opinion has now returned decisively to the later date, 493, for Patrick's death.[32] But if 493 is accurate, then 432 can hardly be. The most likely possibility is that Patrick began his mission in the second half of the fifth century, say, 462.[33]

Patrick makes no mention of his ordination to the priesthood, but the memory of two painful events which occurred some years apart, when he was already a bishop, remained with him. First, there was the kidnapping by Pictish pirates in the service of Coroticus of some members (including women) of a community under Patrick's pastoral care. He had just administered the Sacraments of Christian Initiation to them, when suddenly some were 'put to the sword' and others 'taken captive' (*LC*, 3–4). Second was the contemptuous dismissal of Patrick's emissaries, whom he had sent to Coroticus with an initial letter which,

---

28 See Duffy, *Patrick in His Own Words*, Dublin: Veritas, 2000.

29 '*Lectio divina*' means literally 'sacred reading', a prayerful reading of the Bible.

30 J. B. Bury, *The Life of St Patrick and His Place in History*, London: Macmillan, 1905.

31 See A. P. Smith, *The Earliest Irish Annals: Their First Contemporary Entries and the Earliest Centres of Recording*, Dublin: RIA, 1972.

32 Duffy, *Patrick in His Own Words*, p. 52. See Binchy, 'Patrick and His Biographers'.

33 Binchy, 'Patrick and His Biographers', p. 29, 'To my mind such evidence establishes a presumption that Patrick … cannot have died as early as 461, but must have lived on to the last decade of the fifth century.'

besides registering a sharp protest, also contained proposals to apply customary law in view of a settlement, but to no avail, those to whom the letter was addressed made a mockery of the messengers. This first letter has not survived, but, providentially, we have the second. This second letter is the *Letter to Coroticus*, which will be examined in detail later.

The third stage: Patrick on trial

In the *Confession*, Patrick tells us that as a young boy he committed a sin, 'because I was not yet in control of myself' (*C*, 27). Before being ordained to the diaconate he confessed his sin to a friend, 'a man to whom I entrusted my very soul' (*C*, 32). His friend, who was already a priest, and would later be a bishop, 'had freely and gladly granted me pardon' (*C*, 32). It was this same man who successfully put forward Patrick's name for selection as a bishop, 'Look, you must be raised to the episcopal order' (*C*, 32). Had Patrick a duty to disclose his youthful sin to the prelates who could put his name on a short list for episcopal ordination? At that time in Gaul a penitent, even an officially absolved penitent, could not receive Holy Orders.

It is important to understand the role of the bishop in Patrick's time. Jacques Fontaine, drawing on the preface to Bishop Gennadius's *Statutes of the Ancient Church*, compiled between 476 and 485, notes that 'Bishops played a role of first importance, because they persisted in representing and defending a value system inspired by the very best in their traditions, which were those of a demanding Christianity, renewed and inspired by the monastic ideal, along with those of a nobility holding to its inherited values. Hence too they incarnated and maintained a cultural tradition which preserved and renewed the Latin language, producing thereby a spoken and a written style which enabled a bishop who was also a man of letters (the Statutes prescribed that a bishop should be a *litteratus*), to hand on as living realities the moral, spiritual and even aesthetic values of this heritage.' [34] Patrick claimed to be a nobleman (*LC*, 9), but did his studies and proficiency in Latin come up

34 Jacques Fontaine, 'The Bishop in the Western Church of the Fifth Century', *Seanchas Ard Mhacha (Journal of the Armagh Diocesan Historical Society)*, vol. 16, no. 2, 1995, pp. 1–21.

to the standards proposed here? Even among his brother bishops was he not something of an outsider?

We get the impression that Patrick did not make disclosure and that this worked against him when his youthful sin was brought to light (*C*, 27). The revelation of Patrick's youthful sin could have reduced his legitimate dignity as a bishop to ruins (*C*, 26, 27). Patrick may already have been concerned about his authority as a bishop, due to his interrupted formal education, and we have seen that the issue of his authority as a bishop was central to the writing of the *Letter to Coroticus*. What wounded Patrick most, however, was the betrayal by his friend of the confidence he had placed in him: 'Why did it occur to him afterwards that, before everybody, good and bad, he should put me publicly to shame for a deed for which he had earlier and freely and gladly granted me pardon – as did the Lord, who is greater than all?' (*C*, 32). Is the reference here to Sacramental Absolution? Most scholars say that it is not. But if it was, what Patrick's friend said some years later would have amounted to a violation of the seal of the confessional. That would have been very grave. We also ask, without receiving an answer, what caused this rupture between two churchmen who up until then were such close friends?

Though we lack any official record of the proceedings, it is clear that Patrick was put on trial before a tribunal of inquiry drawn from among his seniors, many of whom were probably also members of the bench of bishops.[35] The indictment, or its equivalent, must have included counts related in some way to the following charges.

The first charge had to do with a sin of his boyhood. We do not know the nature of the offence, but it was deemed of sufficient gravity to render him unfit for the role of bishop. The second charge was probably one of receiving corrupt payments and the misuse of money paid to him for the purposes of the mission in Ireland. Searching for a contemporary comparison, we can think of the corrupt payments made to government ministers or high-ranking government officials in some countries. '*Munera multa mihi offerebantur cum fletu et lacrimis*

---

35 T. M. Charles-Edwards calls it a synod and believes that it was held in Britain. See Charles-Edwards, *Early Christian Ireland*, Cambridge: Cambridge University Press, p. 218.

et offendi illos' (*C*, 37), which translates as 'Many gifts were offered to me with weeping and tears, and I offended them'. The language is the language of rescue and solidarity, but the truth expressed is the 'truth' of power and corrupt influence, which could give access even to kings in Patrick's time.

In answer, Patrick, a man who lived by the truth, categorically denied the accusation of receiving corrupt payments. But is he forthcoming about his debt to God? 'Yes,' he says, 'I am exceedingly in debt to God' (*C*, 38). Patrick was honest in his dealings and truthful in his speech. His integrity was transparent. Let us listen to what he says: 'When I baptised so many thousands of people did I look for even half a screpall from any of them? Give me evidence and I will restore it to you. Or when the Lord ordained clergy everywhere through me, insignificant though I am, and I gave this ministry to them without charge, if I exacted from any of them even the cost of a pair of shoes, speak against me and I will repay you' (*C*, 50). 'On the contrary, I incurred expense for you ... during this period I used to give presents to kings' (*C*, 52). 'In spite of that,' he goes on to say, 'I put myself in grave danger.' He was arrested and at risk of his life. 'I am still spending, and will spend to the limit.' Turning the argument back skillfully on his accusers, he says, 'The Lord is powerful enough to grant me later to spend myself for your souls.'

Nevertheless, he was convicted on all counts. 'I was rejected' (*C*, 29), he says. He had failed the test. His reaction was one of deep hurt and bafflement. There was no more to be said. The decision of the tribunal was a clear expression of 'no confidence' in him personally and in his leadership of the Irish mission. Yet Patrick's conscience was clear.

Patrick goes on to relate that, 'on the day when I was rejected [by my superiors], that night I saw a vision in the night. I looked and before my face was a writing that did not acknowledge my office as a bishop. And as I looked at it I heard a divine voice say to me: "We have seen with disapproval the face of so-and-so," (designated by name). Nor did He say: "You have seen with disapproval", but: "We have seen with disapproval," as if He had associated Himself with me. As He said in Scripture, *He who touches you is as one who touches the apple of my eye.*

That is why I give thanks to Him who in all things gave me strength'
(*C*, 29–30). Patrick is the object of God's special protection and God
sees that justice has not been done.

Patrick had received a heavy blow from an unexpected quarter: his
brother bishops, one of them an intimate friend, 'a man to whom I had
entrusted my very soul'. Duffy observes that a cloud of adverse criticism hung over him for the rest of his life because of what happened.
Tarlach Ó Raifeartaigh believes that the silence concerning Patrick in
the early Irish Church was due to what happened to him on that occasion: 'He was stunned to a point of near despair by the verdict.'[36] He
never really recovered from it. Nevertheless a person who could write
the words that follow does not seem to be a broken person, 'That is
why I give thanks to Him who in all things gave me strength, so that
He did not hinder me from the journey I had decided on, nor from
that work which I had learned from Christ my Lord, but rather I felt in
myself no little power from him, and my fidelity was approved before
God and men' (*C*, 30). Patrick was a man of great Christian fortitude.
T. M. Charles-Edwards believes that in the absence of a metropolitan
archbishop in Ireland, the case was referred to a competent ecclesiastical authority in Britain, or perhaps a synod, by way of appeal.[37] The
outcome was favourable to Patrick but only just.

A key word in this narrative is the Latin word '*defensio*' which occurs
in (*C*, 32), 'at which my defense came up'. But scholars are not agreed
about its meaning. R. C. P. Hanson, Howlett and others believe that
'*defensio*' is to be translated literally. They take it to refer to the court of
inquiry that undoubtedly was set up and sat in judgement on Patrick.
Duffy believes that it is to be translated as 'interdiction' or 'prohibition'.
Ó Raifeartaigh, on the other hand, argues that '*defensio*' does not refer to the 'defense' Patrick makes against the charge of corruption but
refers to a separate inquiry, which took place earlier in Patrick's career,
at which he was appointed bishop-elect. Ó Raifeartaigh argues that
this passage of the *Confession* makes reference to two inquiries. At the
first, before Patrick's trip to Ireland, he is appointed bishop-elect, and

36 Tarlach Ó Raifeartaigh, 'The Enigma of St Patrick', *Seanchas Ardmhacha (Journal of the
    Armagh Diocesan Historical Society)*, vol. 13, no. 2 (1989), pp. 1–60, at p. 37.
37 Charles-Edwards, *Early Christian Ireland*, p. 218.

his close friend speaks in his favour. At the second, which takes place 'mid-career', he is condemned, and his close friend speaks out against him.[38] Elena Malaspina believes that Patrick has borrowed the word '*defensio*' from Paul. She recalls Patrick's admiration for Paul, whom he frequently cites. She gives no legal force to the word '*defensio*' in this context. She refers in this instance first to 1 Corinthians 9:3, 'To those who want to interrogate me, this is my *defensio*, my answer', and then to 2 Timothy 4:16, 'The first time I had to present my defence (*defensio*) no one came into court to support me'. She believes that Patrick was making use of these Pauline texts.[39] I am attracted by Ó Raifeartaigh's reading of '*defensio*'. Unfortunately he cites no source or authority. Malaspina, on the other hand, is probably right in believing that Patrick has relied on Paul, as he does frequently. The divergence of opinion we encounter illustrates the extent of perplexity among the experts with regard to this episode and indeed Patrick's whole life.

Patrick, as we have seen, denied that he was in debt to any human person but was happy to acknowledge that he was very much in debt to God. The great debt he had incurred before God is expressed in Psalm 116:12, 'What return can I make to the Lord for his generosity to me?' The great gift he had received from God was the evangelisation of Ireland. He had already answered his own question. 'This is the return we can make … to exalt and praise God's wonderful deeds before every nation under the whole heaven (*C*, 3). It was a constant theme with Patrick: to praise God and to thank him 'before every nation under the whole heaven'. Psalm 116 was Patrick's canticle of praise and thanksgiving, his Magnificat.

The following additional extracts from the *Confession* clarify further Patrick's attitude to money. They show us his great generosity and integrity. Furthermore, they make it possible to form a concrete idea of the social and political circumstances under which Patrick had to work. Among these were the many missionary journeys he had to make. It is clear that Patrick had access to money and was in a position to pay

---

38   See Tarlach Ó Raifeartaigh, 'St Patrick and the "Defensio"', *Seanchas Ardmhacha (Journal of the Armagh Diocesan Historical Society)*, vol. 11, no. 1 (1983/1984), pp. 22–31.

39   See Elena Malaspina, *Gli scritti di san Patrizio: alle origini del cristianesimo irlandese*, Rome: Edizioni Borla, 1985.

important sums to local kings and governors in order to be allowed to enter their territories for the purpose of preaching there. There are several references: 'I paid out monies for your sake, that they might accept me' (*C*, 51); 'You yourselves know how much I paid out to those who wielded authority throughout the districts I more frequently visited … not less than the price of fifteen men, so that you might have the benefit of my presence, and I might always have the joy of your presence before God. I do not regret it, nor do I count it enough' (*C*, 53); 'All that time I used to give presents to the kings in addition to paying wages to their sons who travelled with me' (*C*, 52); 'I journeyed among you, and everywhere, in your interest, in many dangers, even to the remotest parts beyond which nobody lived, and whither no one had ever come to baptize, or ordain clerics, or confirm the people. By gift of the Lord I did it all with diligence and joy for the sake of your salvation' (*C*, 51).

At the end of the *Confession,* Patrick reiterates the central theme: 'I testify in the Truth', he says, 'and in exultation of heart before God and his holy angels, that I never had any reason other than the Gospel, and its promises, for returning to that race from whom in an earlier time I had barely made good my escape' (*C*, 61). In the last paragraph he makes the following trenchant declaration: 'This is my prayer: that if I have accomplished … any small part of God's plan … the reader may regard it as a true fact to be firmly believed, that is was all the gift of God. And that is my confession before I die' (*C*, 62).

As an elderly man, Patrick knew that his preaching and pastoral ministry in Ireland had borne fruit. He was filled with gratitude. 'I am very much indebted to God who granted me so great a grace that through me a multitudinous people should be reborn for God and afterwards confirmed; they who never had knowledge of God, but up till now worshipped only idols and abominations, have lately been made "a people of the Lord", and are called "children of God"' (C, 41). At the end of the *Letter to Coroticus,* despite the killing and kidnapping of the members of his community, he is still able to say: 'I have not laboured for nothing, nor has my exile (*peregrinatio*) been in vain' (*LC*, 16).

We know that Patrick spent the last years of his life in Ireland and died there. 'Here I am in my old age' (*C*, 10). 'And that is my confession before I die' (*C*, 62). 'I have given up homeland and family, and my life, even unto death – should I be worthy of that. I live for my God, to teach the heathens, even if I am despised by some' (*LC*, 1).

2: Reading the *Letter to Coroticus*

The *Letter to Coroticus* is the earlier of Patrick's two surviving literary compositions. It is highly unusual to find a bishop in antiquity writing a letter without the help of an amanuensis (secretary). This letter was written by Patrick, 'in his own hand' (*LC*, 2). As to its form, it may be described as an 'open letter' intended to be read in public, 'before all the communities' (*LC*, 19), 'even in the presence of Coroticus'. As to its principal purpose, the letter is a decree of excommunication addressed to Coroticus and his men who, though they are Christians, have nevertheless murdered or seized as prisoners members of Patrick's community during or immediately after their baptism or confirmation (*LC*, 3).

Patrick omits the opening greeting customary in ancient letter writing. Even Paul, when writing to rebuke the Galatians, respected this custom (Gal 1:1–4). The omission of the 'salutation' makes the letter unique. It is an expression of the deep feelings that impelled Patrick to make his point at once. It is enough for him simply to present himself and declare his role in society. He begins, 'I, Patrick, a sinner and unlearned, resident in Ireland, declare myself to be a bishop' (*LC*, 1).

Patrick moves quickly to describe what happened. 'The day following that on which the white-robed neophytes had been anointed with chrism – it was still fragrant on their foreheads – they were cruelly put to the sword by those I have named' (*LC*, 3). The Christian community and every God-fearing person are to know that these men, whom Patrick has 'named', are to be excommunicated. Patrick fulfils his duty, though it causes him pain, 'not that I wished anything so harsh and so rough to come from my lips' (*LC*, 1).

It is important to understand the gravity of what has happened. Coroticus and his men are themselves baptised members of the Church.

They have done something terrible to Patrick's community, but they are not 'outsiders'. As Patrick Mullins emphasises, 'because Christ's disciples are one fold (Jn 10) and have one God and Father (Eph 4:6), those who have been baptised constitute one vast corporate body in such a way that if one member suffers, all the members suffer with it.' [40] The crimes of Coroticus and his men constitute apostasy, a betrayal of what they publicly professed on the day of their own baptism.

The popular image of the conversion of Ireland to Christianity is a non-violent one. The *Letter to Coroticus* gives us reason to reconsider this. If Coroticus was motivated by hatred of the faith (*odium fidei*), then should we consider his victims to be proto-martyrs of the Irish Church? Even if Coroticus was not motivated by hatred of the faith, it is clear from the tone of Patrick's letter that the violence experienced by the early Irish Christians significantly marked them.

Patrick's indignation is fierce. By his actions, he says, Coroticus and his men have forfeited the right to be addressed as 'my fellow citizens' or as 'fellow citizen of the holy Romans' (*LC*, 2).[41] Instead, he calls them 'fellow citizens of the demons' – a chilling phrase – 'because of their evil deeds. In enemy fashion they live in death, allies of the Scotti and the apostate Picts' (*LC*, 2).[42] These men, Patrick continues, are 'blood-stained, bloodied with the blood of innocent Christians whom I have begotten in countless numbers unto God, and have confirmed in Christ . . . I sent a letter with a holy priest whom I had taught from his infancy, clerics accompanying him' (*LC*, 2–3).

In accordance with the custom of the Christians of Roman Gaul, Patrick has proposed that Coroticus release his baptised captives (*LC*, 13). In disregard of that custom, Coroticus has mocked Patrick's envoy

---

40   Patrick Mullins, 'The Church as Christ's Body in St Patrick's Letter to Coroticus', in Salvador Ryan and Bishop Brendan Leahy (eds.), *Treasures of Irish Christianity: People and Places, Images and Texts*, Dublin: Veritas, 2012, p. 18.

41   Hanson, *Historical Saint Patrick*, p. 61.

42   Hanson casts light on these words: '"Romans" was a word specially used for citizens of the former Western Roman Empire who either survived in independent enclaves, or who, though under barbarian rule, retained their own culture, language, and system of law. Until at least the ninth century the word Scotti referred to the Irish. The Picts (the painted people) were a race, or perhaps a nation, consisting of several races living in the north east of what is now Scotland. The word "apostate" (a rebel) is used loosely as a term of abuse.'

(*LC*, 3) and brought Patrick's authority as a bishop into question.

Faced with Coroticus's contempt for him, Patrick asserts his authority, 'I am no maker of false claims' (*LC*, 6). Patrick states that he is 'an ambassador' for Christ (*LC*, 5). He uses similar language in the *Confession* (*C*, 56). In this Patrick deliberately echoes Paul (2 Cor 5:20), drawing a comparison between the 'persecution' of Patrick and his community and the persecution suffered by all those 'called and predestined to preach the Gospel' (*LC*, 6). Patrick is a spokesperson for God. Patrick's assertion of his authority is important given what his letter aims to accomplish: the excommunication of Coroticus and his men.

The *Letter to Coroticus* may not be drafted like a formal decree of excommunication, but it is the next best thing. D. S. Nerney, who studied the decree *Inter Ceteras* of Pope Innocent I (401–417), concluded that Patrick possessed the necessary skill in drafting an episcopal decree and was conversant with the 'phraseology and form and style of a decree from an episcopal curia.'[43] The term '*excommunicatio*' does not appear in the letter. Patrick prefers to say that Coroticus and his men are 'foreign' to him and to Christ (*LC*, 5). The latin term is '*alieni*', meaning that Coroticus and his men are estranged from the Christian community. Coroticus and his men will remain estranged from the Christian community until they 'through rigorous penance, unto the shedding of tears, render satisfaction to God, and free the menservants of God and the baptized maidservants of Christ, for whom He died and was crucified' (*LC*, 6).

This expulsion means that Coroticus and his men will no longer be admitted to the celebration of the Eucharist, will not receive hospitality, nor be able to offer it. 'It is not lawful to pay court to such people, or to eat and drink with them ... nor may their alms be accepted' (*LC*, 6).

The *Letter to Coroticus*, though an official communication, is nevertheless highly personal and charged with emotion. Patrick is lonely and isolated, yet he is 'driven by zeal for God' (*LC*, 1). He makes clear his sorrow and distress over the fate that has befallen his people. 'Oh my fairest and fondest brothers and sons ... what shall I do for you?' (*LC*, 15). He expresses his bitter sorrow but remains in control of himself.

43 Conneely, *Letters of Saint Patrick*, p. 182.

He is not carried away by his feelings and is capable of doing what is needed. Even at this early stage, he has some words of mercy for the men guilty of the murder of Patrick's new Christians. If God inspires a spirit of repentance in their hearts, then peace be with them.

The *Letter to Coroticus* and Paul's Letters

I want now to return to the topic of Patrick's relationship with Paul, paying particular attention to the relationship between the *Letter to Coroticus* and Paul's letters.

In 2 Corinthians, Paul is under fire from his critics, who want to displace him, accusing him of spiritual and cultural ineptitude for the apostolate: 'When you see him in person, he makes no impression, and his powers of speaking are negligible' (2 Cor 10:10). Nerney has compared the charges brought against Patrick by his seniors (*C*, 26) to the criticism levelled at Paul.

Paul had already staked out his defensive position in the 1 Corinthians: 'Paul, called to be an apostle of Christ Jesus by the will of God, and our brother Sosthenes, to the church of God in Corinth ...' (1 Cor 1:1–2). He is not one of the Twelve, but the title apostle is not confined to them (Barnabas, for example, is called an apostle in Acts 14:4, 14). Then, in 2 Corinthians, he says, 'But it is God who establishes us with you in Christ and has anointed us, who has put his seal on us and given us his Spirit in our hearts as a down payment' (2 Cor 1:21–22). The allusion to anointing and seal may refer to the gift of the Spirit to the apostolic ministry, but Paul is clear about the basis for his authority. In multiple places he confirms that he is an apostle 'neither by human commission nor from human authorities but through Jesus Christ and God the Father' (Gal 1:1, see also 1 Cor 1:1 and Rom 1:1). His 'vocation' is from God. Divine vocation, not merit, is the basis of his authority.

In the *Letter to Coroticus*, Patrick follows Paul's method of argument. Like Paul, an apostle of Jesus Christ, Patrick declares his apostolic role and position at the very outset: 'I Patrick, a sinner and unlearned, resident in Ireland, declare myself to be a bishop. I believe with complete certainty that it is from God that I received what I am' (*LC*, 1). He reinforces his claim: 'I am no maker of false claims. I have a share with those whom He has called and predestined to preach the Gospel' (*LC*, 6).

Nerney draws attention to the special choice which God made of both Paul and Patrick. Paul says, God 'set me apart before I was born and called me through his grace' (Gal 1:15). He was pre-ordained to fulfil the role God later assigned to him; he says of himself that he was a 'chosen instrument' (Acts 9:15). Both Paul and Patrick were prepared by God for the special work he would entrust to them. Patrick was 'a stone stuck in deep mire' (*C*, 12). He asks, 'Who was it that aroused me, a fool, from the midst of those who are wise … and inspired me?' (*C*, 13). Paul was summoned by a voice from heaven as he made his way to Damascus on a mission to obtain legal authority 'to arrest and take to Jerusalem any followers of the Way' (Acts 9:2). Patrick was called in a dream, 'a vision of the night' while he was on the hills with his sheep (*C*, 17).

Paul tells his readers and critics that he is an ambassador of Jesus Christ (2 Cor 5:20). Ambassadors are accredited representatives of their governments. They both give and receive messages on behalf of those governments. They may be given power to sign treaties as well. They may even be invested with full powers to sign without consultation. It goes without saying that they are immune from the power of the government to which they are sent. In fact their residences and the embassy offices form part of the sovereign territory of their respective nations. They are inviolable. Properly accredited and respected ambassadorial status is uniquely important in the conduct of relations between governments. It is therefore a very serious offence in International Law to violate the diplomatic status of an ambassador who has duly presented their credentials. Paul says that he is God's ambassador, nothing less; he is in effect saying that he can act on behalf of God. He is saying, 'God has conferred authority on me. I have not received it from any human authority.' He has been appointed by God, he is responsible to God, and subject to God's judgement alone.

Patrick too is an ambassador for God, and for 'Christ my God'. Therefore he possesses authority to impose the sanctions (notably excommunication) he refers to in the *Letter to Coroticus*. The fact that

Coroticus and his men have no reverence for God or his bishops does not change the truth of the matter. The guilty parties must make reparation. 'But if God inspires them to return, at some time or another to a right mind towards Him so that even at a late hour they repent of such an impious deed .... , peace be to them' (*LC*, 19). Paul for his part acknowledges that he is a 'vessel of clay' (2 Cor 4:7), easily cracked or shattered. He is no less fragile than any other human being. Yet he holds the Gospel in his hands. It has been entrusted to him.

In defending his authority and the conduct of his office as a bishop Patrick draws on the two Corinthian Letters of Paul, mainly the second. Twice he calls himself 'an ambassador for God', echoing Paul. Paul was subjected to intense criticism at Corinth on various grounds. In reply, he did not claim that he was worthy of the office he held. Instead he affirmed that God had called him to fulfil it. God had called, and God could dismiss. No merit or competence of his had determined God's choice. 'Not that we are qualified of ourselves to claim anything as coming from us; our qualification is from God, who has made us qualified to be ministers of a new covenant' (2 Cor 3:5–6). Patrick takes up the same argument. 'I, Patrick ... declare myself to be a bishop. I believe with complete certainty that it is from God that I have received what I am' (*LC*, 1).

It cannot have been easy for Patrick, but God was with him to vindicate him. He consistently borrows his arguments from Paul, 'You know and God knows how I lived among you' (Acts 20:18). 'I came to the heathen Irish to preach the Gospel and to endure insults from unbelievers; to hear myself taunted for being a foreigner, to experience many persecutions unto bonds; and to surrender my free-born status for the benefit of others' (*C*, 37). Finally in the *Confession*, he makes it clear that, 'if I shall be found worthy of it, I am ready to give even my life unhesitatingly and very gladly for him' (*C*, 37).

Patrick describes himself as a 'stranger and exile' for the love of God. He has renounced everything for the sake of Christ, including his social status. He is like Jesus who, 'though he was rich, yet for your sakes he became poor, so that by his poverty you might become rich' (2 Cor 8:9). Patrick accepted the loss of all things for the sake of Christ and the

Gospel. In this regard he follows the example of Paul, who in Philippians writes of a Christian theology of self-emptying (*kenosis*). The *Letter to Coroticus*, as such, not only demonstrates Patrick's careful reading of Paul's letters but also builds on Paul's theology.

The *Letter to Coroticus*, as well as the *Confession*, is one source of an Irish spirituality characterised by a willingness to embrace life-long exile, radical poverty and renunciation of social status – all for the sake of Christ.

Patrick the exile

We are justified in seeing in Patrick the first exponent of 'exile for the love of Christ' *(peregrinatio ob amorem Christi)* in Irish Christianity. 'Our exile *(peregrinatio)* was not in vain' (*LC*, 16). Again, we see evidence of Patrick's spirituality of self-emptying *(kenosis)*, which echoes Paul in Philippians.

> Let the same mind be in you that was in Christ Jesus,
> who, though he existed in the form of God,
> did not regard equality with God
> as something to be grasped,
> but emptied himself,
> taking the form of a slave,
> assuming human likeness.
> And being found in appearance as a human,
> he humbled himself
> and became obedient to the point of death—
> even death on a cross.
> Therefore God exalted him even more highly ... (Phil 2:5–9)

In 2 Corinthians 5:6–8, Paul, speaking of Christian death, says, 'while we are at home in the body we are away from the Lord'. Our life in this body here on earth is one of exile, a *peregrinatio*, because our true home is in heaven with the Lord. In 1 Peter 1 the recipients of Peter's letter are addressed as 'exiles' *(peregrini)*. The phrase is also found in Psalm 39:12, where the Psalmist describes himself as an 'alien'. The exile had no rights (not unlike the undocumented immigrant). The exile was highly vulnerable and could even be killed with impunity. For that reason the exile was considered to be the object of the special protection of God.

Patrick, who had experienced slavery, was 'raised high' by God. 'I am freeborn by descent: I am the son of a decurion. The fact is that for the benefit of others I sold my freeborn state – I am not ashamed of it, and I have no regrets; in short I am a slave in Christ to a foreign people for the sake of the inexpressible glory of the eternal life which is in Christ Jesus our Lord' (*LC*, 10).

The monk as exile (*peregrinus*) humbled himself radically. This spirituality, rooted in Scripture, was central to the asceticism of the Desert Fathers. The monk's way of life was governed by the ideal of white martyrdom (the giving of one's life to God without bloodshed) ever since the emancipation of the Christians at Rome by the Emperor Constantine in 330, from the time when red martyrdom (the giving of one's life to God with bloodshed) became uncommon.

Parallels

The parallels between Patrick and Paul can be seen in different ways. Patrick may be deliberately imitating Paul, modelling his own defence of his authority as a bishop on Paul's. The parallels may be biographical, in that the lives of the two men may simply resemble one another as a matter of fact. Finally, the parallels may be spiritual. Insofar as Paul and Patrick share in the same spiritual task, the spread of the Gospel, they resemble one another.

The *Letter to Coroticus* can be read not only as an historical document, shedding light on an important event in the life of Patrick, but as a literary treatment of Pauline themes of pastoral authority and the Christian life.

3: Reading the *Confession*

This chapter explores the *Confession* in greater depth, bearing in mind the literary form to which it belongs and with fuller awareness of the strong patristic influences to which the author was subject. This chapter is not a systematic commentary. There are several such already. Rather I intend to read through the text listening attentively to what Patrick is saying, paying particular attention to those moments when he opens his heart to God and to the reader. First, however, it is necessary to explore both the literary form of the *Confession* and the patristic influences that affected Patrick.

The confessional form

A literary form is a recognised category or class of writing governed by generally accepted rules and conventions. For example, a newspaper report of a rugby match and the entries in a personal diary belong to different literary forms and are very different. Patrick's *Confession* can be said to belong to the confessional form.

The exemplar of the confessional form is Augustine's *Confessions*. The confessional form is marked broadly by a restless pursuit or search for truth that concerns itself primarily with the inner life of the human being. It can be autobiographical but may be light on factual detail, focusing instead on what the author thought or felt about particular events.

The confessional form has a long history closely tied to both religion and philosophy. Cicero (106–43 BC) identified the turn toward the human being in Greek philosophy with Socrates (470–399 BC): 'Socrates was the first to call philosophy down from the heavens and set her into the cities of men, and bring her into their homes, and compel her to ask questions about life and morality, and things good and evil.'[44] Instead of focusing on questions about the nature of the physical uni verse, as many 'pre-Socratic' philosophers had done, Socrates turned toward questions about the life of the human being. He pursued truth and knowledge by examining and interrogating his own inner life and the inner lives of others. In a religious context, this pursuit of truth became the pursuit of God.

Justin Martyr (AD 100–165) detailed his own path from studying philosophers like Plato and Socrates to embracing the truth of Christianity. Justin Martyr identified the prophets of the Old Testament, like Moses, as influences on Greek philosophy and as more 'esteemed' and 'ancient' than the Greek philosophers.[45]

The Psalms influenced the development of the confessional form, especially in the case of Augustine. In the Psalms we find the origins of *confessio laudis* (confession of praise) and *confessio peccati* (confession of sin). Psalms 111–113 are known as the 'Hallelujah Psalms'. They celebrate and praise God. 'Paise the Lord! I will give thanks to the Lord with my whole heart' (Ps 111). Augustine would have been familiar with the 'Penitential Psalms' (Ps 6, 32, 38, 51, 102, 130, 143), which concern sin and failure. 'Happy are those whose transgression is forgiven, whose sin is covered' (Ps 32).

These two strands, the biblical and the classical, would come together to shape the confessional form, particularly in the case of Augustine's *Confessions*.

Patrick and the confessional form

Scholars do not agree about the employment of the confessional form in Patrick. While Augustine used the plural 'confessions' in the title of his book, Patrick used the singular 'confession'. Mohrmann suggests that while Augustine's title refers to multiple uses of the term '*confessio*', Patrick's may not even be intended as a title.[46] Mohrmann argues that Patrick uses the term '*confessio*' in the sense of the expression 'testimony of our conscience', which is found in Paul (2 Cor 1:12): 'There is one

---

44 Cicero, *Tusculan Disputations* (V 4, 11). See also Plato, *Phaedo* (96ff).
45 Justin Martyr, *First Apology* and *Dialogue with Trypho*.
46 Mohrmann, *Four Lectures*, p. 5.

thing we are proud of, namely the "testimony of our conscience" that we have always behaved towards everyone, and especially towards you, with that unalloyed holiness that comes from God.' In contrast, Augustine uses the term '*confessio*' in three interrelated ways: *confessio peccati* (confession of sin)*, confessio laudis* (confession of praise)*, confessio fidei* (confession of faith).

Mohrmann goes on to say that Patrick's work is more than an apology, it is rather an explanation and an account of his missionary work. At the same time there is an element of self-examination in it. Patrick is reviewing and meditating on his life's work; he wants to leave a legacy. For Mohrmann, one thing is clear: it is not the *Confessions* of Augustine but the *testimonium* of Paul that is to be seen behind the *Confession* of Patrick.[47]

The dramatic ending phrase used by Patrick in the *Confession*, 'before I die', makes it akin to a 'farewell discourse', like that of Jesus to his disciples at the Last Supper (Jn 13–17) or that of Paul to the elders of the Church at Ephesus (Acts 20:17–38). A farewell discourse can be confessional. Even if Mohrmann is correct in identifying Patrick's '*confessio*' as following after Paul rather than Augustine, this does not preclude Patrick's *Confession* belonging as a whole to the confessional form. Conneely argues that even if Patrick does not use the term '*confessio*' in the relevant ways, confessions of sin, faith and praise are undeniably thematically present in Patrick.[48]

Patrick and Augustine

Finan[49] remarks that in the confessional form facts (in the sense of the external events of a life) are not the principal point of the exercise. The facts will not be exhaustive but will be selected with respect to their significance to the author. As the reader will quickly realise, the *Confession* contains relatively few facts but is rich in reflection and interior depth.

Finan considers that the greatest confessions are those of the greatest converts, and the cases of Patrick and Augustine clearly justify this view.

---

47 Mohrmann, *Four Lectures*, p. 6.
48 Conneely, *Letters of Saint Patrick*, p. 133.
49 See Conneely, *Letters of Saint Patrick*, pp. 131–135, on which I depend for much of my discussion of *confessio* as a literary genre/form.

Nor is it surprising that the greatest confessions are written by authors who temperamentally are 'pilgrims of the absolute', who possess the Augustinian restless heart, whose writing is characterised by passionate questioning of existence. People who, like Augustine, know that their hearts are pilgrims and can find rest only in God. They journey onwards sustained by the hope of finding and entering the city of God: 'You have made us for yourself, and our hearts are restless until they rest in you' (Augustine's *Confessions,* I, 1).

In Augustine's *Confessions* the word '*confessio*' occurs in three combinations: confession of sin, confession of praise, and confession of faith. Though the emphasis varies from place to place, confession of sin nearly always implies confessions of faith and praise, and likewise each of the three implies the other two.[50] In the context of the confessional form, a confession is always a public declaration, addressed to God in the first place, but also to men and women. Augustine says, 'I confess not only before you … but also in the ears of the believing sons of men' (Augustine's *Confessions*, X: 4, 6).

A confession in the formal sense is also an account of events whose truth is vouched for by the person who has lived through them. These are narrated so that an Augustine or a Patrick can awaken in the soul of the reader the religious search which he himself has known so as to arouse in the reader a movement of conversion and return to God, saying in effect: 'I bear witness that this is what God has done for me. God will do it for you too if you ask humbly, for God is generous and rich in mercy.'

Patrick himself offers a good description of what confession involves. With the Psalmist he asks, 'What return can we make to the Lord for all that he has done for us?' (*C*, 3; Ps 116:12). He answers, 'This is the return we can make after God corrects us and brings us to know him: to exalt and praise his wonderful deeds before every nation under the whole heaven' (*C*, 3). At the conclusion of the *Confession* (*C*, 61–62), Patrick twice uses the term '*confessio*' to describe what he has just written: 'Here then one more time let me set down the theme of my *confes-*

---

50 John J. O'Meara, *The Young Augustine*: *An Introduction to the Confessions of St Augustine*, London: Longmans, 1980.

sio', and 'It was all the gift of God. And that is my *confessio* before I die.'[51]

The New Testament contains many exemplars of confession that Patrick would have known. Jesus says, 'I confess to you, Father', i.e., 'I praise you, Father, Lord of heaven and earth, because you have hidden these things from the wise and intelligent and have revealed them to infants' (Mt 11:25). Peter confesses, 'You are the Messiah, the Son of the living God' (Mt 16:16), which earns him the praise of Jesus. In John's Gospel the man born blind confesses to those who ask him how he has been cured (Jn 9:1–12). In Romans we find, 'if you confess with your mouth that Jesus is Lord and believe in your heart that God raised him from the dead, you will be saved' (Rom 10:9).

One area where Patrick and Augustine clearly differ is in regard dialogue with God. In Augustine's *Confessions* he talks, explains, discusses, asks questions and wonders. He could be said to 'chat' with God. Everywhere in the Augustine's *Confessions* there is an invisible partner in dialogue, an interlocutor, God himself. This is not generally a feature of Patrick's work. The exception is when Patrick asks God, 'Who am I, Lord, or what is my calling? You who helped my work with such divine power that today among the nations I steadfastly exalt and glorify Your Name wherever I am …' (*C*, 34).

If we examine Patrick's own account of his motive for writing the *Confession*, we find a common thread that runs through Augustine and back to the classical tradition. Patrick declares that he writes, 'In order that my brethren may know the kind of man I am and perceive the desire of my soul' (*C*, 6). On the lintel of the door of the Temple of Apollo at Delphi the words 'Know thyself' were carved. Knowledge of God, of self, and one's deep desire were the key elements in the programme of Platonic philosophy. In the *Soliloquies*[52] Augustine asks himself, 'What do you want to know?' He replies, 'I want to know God and the soul.'

---

51 Finan argues convincingly that it is natural that the great confessions should centre upon the two great poles of reality. 'I desire to know God and my soul' writes Augustine in the first book of the Soliloquies I 2, 7. The supposedly rustic Patrick asks: 'Who am I Lord, or, what is my calling, that you have made known such divine power to me?' (*C*, 34). Finan goes on to say that it is within and from this larger theme that there arise those more specific motifs of confession that we mentioned earlier, confession of sin, of praise, and of faith. It is the Augustinian pattern and the Patrician pattern too. See Conneely, *Letters of Saint Patrick*, p. 134–5.

52 Augustine, *Soliloquies and the Immortality of the Soul*, I,7.

Patrick's concern with self-knowledge and care of the soul could point to a knowledge of the philosophy of Augustine.[53]

The style and structure of the *Confession*

The complaints often made about Patrick's writing arise in part from the focus of scholars on the search for factual detail in the *Confession* (as well as the *Letter to Coroticus*). In a fundamental insight, Howlett has demonstrated that these complaints mostly arise from a failure to appreciate Patrick's literary style. Patrick's apparent goal is to write 'biblical' Latin with a patristic colouring. This he achieves with great success.[54] Essential to Patrick's literary style is the use of chiasmus. A chiasmus is an arrangement of the form ABBA. Consider, for example, the opening lines of the *Confession*.

A *Ego* Patricius peccator	*I am Patrick, a sinner*
B *Patrem* habui Calpornium	*My father was Calpornius*
B Villulam enim prope habuit *(pater)*	*(My father) had a small estate near by*
A Ubi *ego* capturam dedi	*Here I was captured*

A *Annorum* habui *fere sedecim*	I was just sixteen years old
B *Deum* enim verum ignorabam	I did not know the true God
B Quia a *Deo* recessimus	We had abandoned God
A Deus misertus est *adolescentiae meae*	God had pity on *my youthfulness*

If we read the *Confession* superficially, it may strike us as poorly structured, but if we read it more attentively, we can see that Patrick has in fact ordered his material. Hanson says, 'There is a certain wholeness and completed design in Patrick's *Confession* which prevents it from being a mere desultory stringing together of unconnected remarks.' According to Hanson the *Confession* falls easily into five parts:

---

53 Karl Rahner, *Foundations of Christian Faith*, 'The Knowledge of God', London: Darton Longman and Todd, 1984, p. 51.
54 For a detailed account of chiasmus in Patrick see Howlett, *The Book of Letters of St Patrick the Bishop*.

I.   Youth, capture, God's goodness to him (*C*, 1–15)
II. Escape from Ireland to Britain (*C*, 16–22)
III. Other manifestations of God's care (*C*, 23–34)
IV. The fruits of his ministry in Ireland (*C*, 35–55)
V.   Conclusion (*C*, 56–62).

Hanson believes that this division brings out the coherence and balance of the book.[55]

We have already seen that it was never Patrick's intention to write a full-blown autobiography. Accordingly, he gives few concrete details about his life. If he included some, it was mainly because he wished to give public testimony concerning his inner journey and to give thanks to God for his role in helping him to complete it. Bearing in mind the differences of opinion among scholars, how then should we approach the *Confession*? The primary meaning of the Latin word '*confessio*' is an 'acknowledgement', a 'formal admission', a 'declaration'.[56] Secondary meanings include: 'a revelation of oneself', or 'a manifestation of oneself'. We will not go far wrong if we remember these primary and secondary meanings. When applied to a piece of writing, they indicate that the reader should expect to find in it an account of the writer's inner life, an apology or a defense of his life, his search for God, his encounter with God, praise of God, his moral and religious struggles. The *Confession* is obviously not a letter, at least in the ordinary sense, but if it is not accurate to describe it as an autobiography either, then what is it? Patrick simply calls it his '*confessio*': 'This is my *confessio* before I die' (*C*, 62). If we take the autobiographical elements into account, we can define it more exactly as 'confessional-autobiographical' in form, which if not elegant, is at least accurate.[57]

The spiritual journey of the *Confession*

In writing the *Confession,* Patrick wishes to reveal himself and express his gratitude to God. We can sense his profound faith and his deep intimacy with God. He really knows and loves God. He has another

55 Hanson, *Historical Saint Patrick*, pp. 41–42.
56 *Chambers Murray Latin–English Dictionary*.
57 See Conneely, *The Letters of Saint Patrick*, p. 131.

major reason for writing: to refute the defamatory claims made against him. The *Confession* is Patrick's defense of the way he has lived his life. As we have seen, scholars like Mohrmann compare Patrick at this point with 2 Corinthians 1:12 of Paul, where Paul speaks of his conscientious conviction that he has always behaved towards his people with that unalloyed holiness that comes from God.

Confession 1–15

The key time in the life of Patrick was the period of his captivity. It was *kairos* (2 Cor 6:4), the acceptable time, the time of grace. To quote Patrick, 'then I earnestly sought God and there I found him' (*C*, 33). Everything is contained in this. We read in Jeremiah, 'When you search for me, you will find me; if you seek me with all your heart' (Jer 29:13), and in Isaiah, 'Seek the Lord while he may be found, call upon him while he is near' (Isa 55:6). This was the core teaching of Ignatius of Loyola: searching for and finding God in all things. Patrick too turned to God and that made all the difference.

God first prepared Patrick by chastising him. 'I know not, God knows, if I was then fifteen years old, and I did not believe in the living God, nor had I believed in him from childhood, but remained in death and unbelief until I was severely chastised and truly humbled by hunger and nakedness – and that, daily' (*C*, 27). In Hebrews we learn the meaning of divine chastisement, 'for the Lord disciplines those whom he loves and chastises every child whom he accepts' (Heb 12:6).

The gifts God bestowed on Patrick after this conversion included the gifts of faith, of repentance, of pardon for his sins, of protection and divine consolation. By the grace of God, Patrick grew in these divine gifts to him, in the love and fear of God, in prayer and in faith. 'I cannot remain silent about such great favours and so great a grace as the Lord deigned to bestow on me in the land of my captivity. Because this is the return we can make after God corrects us and brings us to know him: to exalt and praise his wonderful deeds before every nation under the whole heaven' (*C*, 3).

The opening part of the *Confession* comes to a triumphant climax at section twelve. Patrick tells how God transformed his life. 'I was like a stone lying in deep mud. Then He who is mighty came and in his mercy lifted me aloft and placed me on the top of the wall' (*C*, 12). Patrick knows himself specially chosen by God. Like Paul he is a chosen vessel, a man specially picked out and entrusted with a mission by God.

We think of it in 'before' and 'after' language. It is one of the great declarations of the *Confession*. God's intervention has transformed Patrick's life totally. Now he intends to proclaim from the rooftops what God has done for him. He will speak, even if 'lordly and clever men of letters' (*C*, 13) do not approve. Public praise for the wonders God has done in the life of the author is the essence of confession.

Parallels

Chapter 40 of Isaiah is the beginning the so-called 'Book of Consolation'. It is attributed to a prophet writing in Babylon. Biblical scholars name him 'Second Isaiah'. Speaking of the exiles from Jerusalem living in Babylon, the Lord, through his prophet, says, 'Speak tenderly to Jerusalem, and cry to her that she has served her term, that her penalty is paid' (Isa 40:2). Patrick's experience in captivity can be interpreted in the light of the experience of the people of Jerusalem while they were in Babylon. Both were comforted by God, both were protected by God, both were taught by God and both, under the guidance of God, were finally able to return home.

Another helpful perspective on Patrick's capture and enslavement is provided by the story of Joseph in Genesis (37:2–50:26). Joseph is the object of his brothers' envy because his father has a special love for him. He is a dreamer of dreams, an additional cause of envy on the part of his brothers. Patrick too, we know, is a dreamer. The brothers of Joseph conspire against him to sell him to slave traders. He goes down to Egypt and is sold to Potiphar, one of the Pharaoh's officials. But God protects him, he prospers and becomes chief advisor to the Pharaoh. He avoids various dangers, not least the seductive overtures of Potiphar's wife. Finally, when famine reduces the land of Canaan to dire straits, he becomes the saviour of his father and brothers. It is all in God's plan. Like Joseph, Patrick will experience enslavement, but he too will be protected by God and will in time become saviour of the

Irish people.

A comparison with Ignatius of Loyola is also helpful. The young Basque nobleman had been humiliated in his pride and vanity when he was severely injured in both legs at the siege of Pamplona and was taken prisoner by the French. At this moment of crisis and breakdown God intervened in his life. He was now taught directly by God. During those months from his sickbed to his time in Manresa, 'God dealt with me in the same way that a good teacher deals with the child he/she is teaching.'[58] God introduced him into a much deeper experience of prayer, taught him to pay attention to the signs of his presence and revealed to him the principles of spiritual discernment. Just as the teacher is patient and repeats the lesson until he or she is confident that the pupil has grasped the lesson, so now God taught Patrick personally and with inexhaustible patience. Patrick tells us that while he was caring for sheep out on a hill, God bestowed on him the gift of faith and formed him in the habit of prayer. 'More and more the fear of God and the love of him came to me, and my faith was increased, and my spirit was so moved that on one day I would pray as many as a hundred times, and in the night nearly as often' (*C*, 16). To use another Ignatian expression, Patrick acquired 'familiarity with God' by living in his presence through virtually continuous personal prayer, fulfilling the command of Paul, 'Pray in the Spirit at all times in every prayer and supplication' (Eph 6:18).

Confession 16–22

Paul tells us that when we do not know how to pray, the Spirit prays within us. Patrick prayed to the heavenly Father in the Spirit out on the hillside day and night, in snow, in frost, in rain. He says, 'I felt no ill effects from it, nor was there any sluggishness in me, such as I now see there is, because then the Spirit was fervent in me' (*C*, 16). It is clear that Patrick, who knew the heavenly Father and Our Lord Jesus Christ intimately, also experienced the presence and action of the Holy Spirit in prayer in an exceptionally profound way.

Patrick managed to escape from Ireland, but found himself tested as

---

58 Ignatius of Loyola, *Personal Writings,* 'Reminiscences', Penguin Classics, 1998, p. 25.

he spent twenty-eight days journeying through 'deserted country' (*C*, 19). Just after the miraculous appearance of a herd of pigs that saved several men from starvation (*C*, 19), Patrick experienced a moment of severe trial, 'Satan fell upon me like a huge rock' (*C*, 20). Patrick in his distress called out to Christ, the true Sun, 'While this was happening I saw the sun rise in the heavens, and as I was crying out, "Helias, Helias" with all my strength, lo, the splendour of that sun fell on me ... and I believe that I was aided by Christ my Lord, and that his Spirit was even then crying out on my behalf' (*C*, 20).

In the early Church Elijah was regarded as an Old Testament saint, and it was quite common to invoke Christ the true Sun, *Christos Helios*, by calling out the words, 'Elia, Elia', which in fact are an invocation of the prophet Elijah. Elijah and the rising sun, which stood for Christ, became associated. The 'True Sun' (*Sol Verus*) who is Christ was particularly celebrated at Christmas in place of the 'Unconquered Sun' (*Sol Invictus*), worshipped at the mid-winter festival celebrated by the pagans. Another title for Christ was 'Sun of Justice' (from the Latin *Sol Justitiae*).

When Patrick turned to Christ for help, he knew that the Spirit was even then crying out to God on his behalf. He prays that the Spirit will help him and speak on his behalf 'on the day of his distress'. In a reference to Matthew 10:20, he hopes that on that day, 'it is not you [the disciple] who speak, but the Spirit of your Father speaking through you' (*C*, 20).

Just as they ran out of food, Patrick and his travelling companions found 'human habitation' (*C*, 22).

Parallels

Just as God led the people of Israel out of slavery in Egypt and fed them in the desert, so too God led Patrick out of slavery into a desert and there fed him. Just as Satan put Jesus to the test in the desert, so too he put Patrick to the test in a desert. This episode in Patrick's life is reminiscent of the great temptation of Anthony of Egypt recounted by Athanasius in his *Life of Anthony*. The demons came to Anthony in the cave to attack him. All of a sudden a bright light flashed, and the demons ran away. Anthony knew that the light must have come from God, and he asked God where he was before, when the demons attacked him. God replied, 'I was here but I would see and abide to see thy battle, and because thou hast manly fought and well maintained thy battle, I shall make thy name to be spread through all the world'. Satan also came to Jesus and was duly rebuffed, 'Begone, Satan.' He falls upon Patrick like a great rock, but Patrick is able to withstand him because Jesus intervenes to help him. Jesus overcame Satan, and Anthony and Patrick were helped by Jesus Christ to overcome Satan. It is possible that Patrick read the *Life of Anthony* and felt a connection with Anthony's experience.

Confession 56–62

We read that Patrick is ready to give his life for God, 'If in my life I have ever achieved any good for the cause of my God whom I love, I ask him to let me shed my blood ... Even if I should go without burial itself, or my wretched remains be divided, limb by limb, among dogs or wild beasts, or should birds of the air devour them' (*C*, 59). These are the elements of red martyrdom (the giving of one's life for God with the shedding of blood). Earlier in the *Confession*, Patrick speaks of life among the heathen Irish (*C*, 37). He says that he is unhesitatingly ready to give even his life for the sake of God's name, and he desires to spend his life in Ireland until he dies. These are the elements of white martyrdom (the giving of one's life for God without the shedding of blood). We have already seen elements of white martyrdom in the *Letter to Coroticus* (see p. 48) and understand how it informs Patrick's spirituality of self-emptying.

Patrick's words are reminiscent of one of the Apostolic Fathers, Ignatius, bishop of Antioch. In his *Letter to the Romans*, Ignatius writes, 'I am truly in earnest about dying for God ... I implore you, do me no (such) untimely kindness; pray leave me to be a meal for the beasts, for it is they who can provide my way to God'. At the time of writing, Ignatius was travelling under guard to Rome, where he would indeed be martyred by being fed to beasts. Jerome testifies to this in his *On Illustrious Men*. Andrew Cain argues that Patrick was familiar with the letters of Jerome.[59] It is possible that Patrick's reference to 'wild beasts' is intended to echo Ignatius. Though Mohrmann does not agree, it seems that Patrick was familiar with the writing of Ignatius or perhaps with someone who wrote about Ignatius, like Jerome.

Let us go back for a moment to that powerful overture that opens the *Confession* before looking at the *Confession's* equally moving conclusion. 'I am Patrick, a sinner, unlettered, the least of all the faithful, held in contempt by a great many people' (*C*, 1). We sense that we are in the presence of a man who has a natural gift for powerful expression even though he has never studied the rules of rhetoric, but there is also deep pain in his words. He tells us right away that he is 'held in contempt by many people'. He is very hurt by that, and he believes it to be un-justified. From what we have read about Patrick and his superiors, we already know something about these matters: Patrick's unjust dismiss-al, his deep disappointment at the behaviour of his intimate friend in whom he confided but who betrayed his confidence, the accusations of avarice, ambition and self-enrichment; the questioning of his overall conduct of his office in the missionary outreach of the Romano-British Church to Ireland, first as a priest, then as a missionary bishop; and the unseen motivation (probably Pelagian) which lay behind these and other defamatory attacks on him.

'I now commend my soul to my most faithful God, for whom I am an ambassador in my lowliness. He is no accepter of persons, and for this office he chose me from among his least ones, that I should be one of his ministers' (*C*, 56). The concluding sections of Patrick's *Confession* are brief, but they constitute a kind of spiritual testament. They express the final sentiments of a man who knows that death is near. We have examples of spiritual testaments in recent times from Pope St John XXIII, Pope Blessed Paul VI and Pope St John Paul II.

He began the *Confession* with a clear, authoritative confession of faith (*C*, 4), in which the Christological teaching of the Council of Nicea was adopted with enthusiasm. At the conclusion of his *Confession*, Pat-rick returns to Christology, bringing his glorification of the Trinity to

---

59   Andrew Cain, 'Patrick's "Confessio" and Jerome's "Epistula" 52 to Nepotian', *Journal of Medieval Latin*, vol. 20, 2010, pp. 1–15.

a climax in a powerful 'doxology' (hymn or formula ascribing glory to God). Patrick stresses the glory of Christ, whom he describes as the 'true Sun' (*C*, 60). 'We shall rise on that day in the glory of the Sun: that is to say, in the glory of Christ Jesus our Redeemer … destined to be conformed to his image … We are a people who believe in the true Sun and adore Him, Christ who will never perish. And neither will he who does his will; but he will abide forever, as Christ abides forever, He who with God the Almighty Father and with the Holy Spirit reigns before all ages, as now, and forever and ever (*C*, 59–60).

Patrick returns finally to the central truth that he reiterates throughout the *Confession*: 'This is my prayer, that if I have accomplished or brought to light any small part of God's purpose, none shall ever assert that the credit is due to my own uneducated self, but regard it rather as a true fact to be firmly believed: that it was all the gift of God. And this is my confession before I die' (*C*, 62).

Although Patrick never became a great Latin stylist, studies are making it clearer that he wrote not classical Latin but a vigorous late Latin with strong influences from biblical and patristic Latin.[60] There are, however, things far more important than the ability to write polished Latin that Patrick did achieve, or rather, that God achieved in Patrick, namely his missionary work in Ireland. Reflecting on it all, Patrick says, 'This is my prayer: that if I have accomplished or brought to light any small part of God's plan … *let all* regard it as a true fact firmly to be believed: that it was all the gift of God' (*C*, 62).[61]

---

60 See especially Bieler, *Libri Epistularum Sancti Patricii Episcopi*, Dublin: RIA, 1952, Part II 'Commentary'; Mohrmann, *Four Lectures*; Howlett, *Saint Patrick the Bishop*; and Finan, 'St Patrick's Latinity' in Conneely, *Letters of Saint Patrick*.
61 I have inserted the words in italics. The context suggests this addition.

Part 2:
Patrick: His Legacy

4: Patrick and the Fathers of the Church

'Every time a Christian renewal has blossomed in our West, whether in thought or in life (and the two are always linked), it has blossomed under the sign of the Fathers.'
Henri de Lubac

The period from the second century to the middle of the eighth century is known as the 'Age of the Fathers', i.e., the patristic age.[62] Within the patristic age there is a period known as 'the golden age of patristic writing'. It runs roughly from the middle years of the life of Athanasius (296–373) to the death of Augustine (354–430). The golden age of patristic writing is close to the time of Patrick's life and mission, if, along with most scholars, we accept 462 for the beginning of his mission and 491 for his death.

According to Vincent of Lérins (died c. 445), 'The Fathers are those witnesses of Christian Antiquity who each in his own time and locality were accredited doctors of the Faith in communion with the Church'. Conneely raises the question of which school of theology in the history of the Church best served the mission of the Church. Was it perhaps scholastic theology? But scholastic theology is often abstract and technical, whereas patristic theology is pastorally focused in a way that cannot be said of scholastic theology. Patristic theology is accompanied by prayerful reading of Scripture and keeps the subject matter well focused and in view. Despite the fact that we possess no factual information about Patrick's time in Lérins (assuming that he indeed studied there), it is nevertheless

---

62   The lifetime of St Patrick therefore falls within the patristic period.

reasonable to believe that at that stage of his intellectual and spiritual development, he may have begun to read the Fathers of the Church. The Fathers are especially distinguished for: (a) orthodoxy, (b) holiness of life, (c) recognition by the Church. They are of special authority when they teach a doctrine by unanimous consent, for then they can be taken to be transmitting and bearing witness to the teaching of the Church.[63]

The Second Vatican Council says, 'The words of the holy Fathers bear witness to the living presence of this Tradition, whose wealth is poured into the practice and life of the believing and praying Church.'[64]

A later document published by the Congregation for Catholic Educationsays, 'The Fathers may be considered the true builders of the Church, the creators and promoters of certain indispensable structures of the Church's order, as also of culture and of a style of life that is completely new, specifically Christian, and corresponding to the spirit of the Gospel.'[65]

Pope St John Paul II reminds us, 'In the great era of the Fathers of the Church, saintly bishops devoted an important part of their ministry to catechesis [instruction in the Christian faith]. St Cyril of Jerusalem, St John Chrysostom, St Ambrose and St Augustine, wrote catechetical works that remain models for us.'[66]

Who are the other Fathers? I will list some of the better known: Cyprian of Carthage, Jerome, translator of the Vulgate Bible, Irenaeus of Lyons, Paulinus of Nola and Prosper of Aquitaine. We have mentioned a total of only eight, but they are the most important.

Given that almost all the Fathers were bishops, it is no surprise to see that they wrote to teach, guide and correct their flocks. If we exclude polemics and controversy, their writings consist of sermons, exhortations and letters to guide and illuminate the faithful. Take for example,

63 K. Rahner & H. Vorgrimler, *Concise Theological Dictionary*, Second Edition, London: Burns and Oates, 1983.

64 *Dei Verbum*, Vatican: The Holy See, 1965, 8. See *Catechism of the Catholic Church*, Vatican: The Holy See, p. 19.

65 Congregation for Catholic Education, *Instruction on the Study of the Fathers of the Church in the Formation of Priests*, 1989.

66 Pope John Paul II, *Catechesi Tradendae (Catechesis in our Time)*, Vatican: The Holy See, 1979, 12.

Augustine: he tried to put all theology, including the mystery of the Trinity, within the reach of ordinary people. This direct and concrete theology, open to everyone, which is the fruit of spiritual experience rather than speculation, is an asset that makes patristic theology worth its weight in gold.

Many Greek Fathers, above all, inhabited the cultural milieu of the Bible. For example, as French theologian Adalbert Hamman tells us, the Latins translate a clause in the Lord's Prayer as, 'Forgive us our trespasses as we forgive … ' but in accordance with the Greek text, where the verb is in the past tense, the Greeks translate, 'Forgive us our trespasses as we have forgiven those who trespass against us … ' A whole theology stems from this difference in translation.

The doctrine of the faith had to be preserved, developed, transmitted safely and protected against distortion and the ravages of heresy, especially so after the death of the last apostle. The writings of the Fathers are the earliest writings that are not part of the New Testament, but they constitute the special formative stage of second generation life in the Church.

The office of teaching the true or orthodox doctrine of the faith in the face of heresy belongs to the Church, which is 'the pillar and the ground of truth' (1 Tim 3:15). The exercise of the Sacred Magisterium devolves upon the pope and the bishops. Though the teaching activity of the Fathers as such is distinct from the official teaching office of the Church very many of them were in fact bishops.

The Fathers bear witness to a Church that was still undivided. Consider, for example, the influence exercised by Origen (c. 185–c. 253), who wrote in Greek, upon Ambrose (c. 339–397), who wrote in Latin. We still have the letter of congratulations from Basil (330–378/79), bishop of Caesarea Mazaca in modern-day Turkey, to Ambrose, when he learned that Ambrose had been appointed to the See of Milan. The Greeks have a more philosophical outlook and a richer philosophical vocabulary. The Latins are better jurists and administrators. Here we have different temperaments, and this variety gives patristic theology its richness. There is no route towards reunion with the Orthodox churches that does not lead through a deepening of this common heritage.[67]

Among the early Fathers were Ignatius, bishop of Antioch, martyred c. 107, and Justin Martyr (c. 100–165), whose death took place under Emperor Marcus Aurelius. Another famous name is Polycarp, bishop of Smyrna, who was martyred in 155. He had personally known John the Apostle and was therefore a most important link between the time of the Apostles and the earliest Christian Fathers. Polycarp opposed the errors of the Gnostics. Irenaeus, bishop and martyr (c. 120/140–c. 202/203), himself a great opponent of the Gnostics, had known Polycarp in his youth and was much influenced by him.

In the West the four great Fathers and Doctors of the Church were Ambrose (c. 339–397), Augustine (354–430), Jerome (c. 345–420), and Gregory (c. 540–604). Among these, only Jerome was not a bishop.

Patrick and the Fathers

The scholars who compiled the index to Conneely's book, *The Letters of Saint Patrick*, tell us that references are traceable in Patrick's *Confession* and *Letter to Coroticus* to at least twenty of the Church Fathers. Most prominent among them are Augustine and Hilary of Poitiers.[68] We have already made reference to Ignatius of Antioch and been struck by the affinity between the bishop of Antioch and Patrick (see page 60). This should leave us able to claim credibly that Patrick was well versed in patristic theology and ought to be included by the Church among the Fathers.

Conneely held a very high opinion of Patrick's knowledge both as a student and later as a bishop. He writes, 'A preliminary but careful study of the writings, in the context of patristic literature and law, establishes Patrick as a patristic theologian and churchman of competence, and of great intellectual stature'.[69] It can be argued that a thorough appraisal of Patrick is now due from theologians who specialise in early patrology.

---

67   Adalbert Hamman, *How to Read the Church Fathers,* London: SCM Press, 1993.
68   Others include: Ambrose, Arnobius, Bonifatius, Cyprianus Carthaginensis, Jerome, Innocenius, Irenaeus, Novatianus, Paulinus Nolanus, Prosper of Aquitane.
69   Conneelly, *Letters of Saint Patrick*, p. 199.

Conneely says, 'We find [in Patrick's writings] a process and a form of theological thought which is typically patristic, i.e., reflexion within the presencing of God in faith-life. Such reflexion is fully personal. It includes both discernment and responsiveness, both insight and affect, both light and warmth. It articulates itself both in doctrinal truths and in prayerful attitudes. Its idiom is predominantly that of Sacred Scripture which is quoted extensively and also echoed in it. All these qualities are present, to a remarkable degree, in St Patrick. Indeed, although his extant writings are no more than an open pastoral letter and a letter of excommunication, when one compares these texts with the patristic literature of his time, one sees how well versed he was in patristic theology and how typical an exponent he was of it in content, style and method.'

We can now consider the relationship between Patrick and several of the Fathers individually, focusing not only on a textual point of view but also from the point of view of the theological connections between Patrick and the Fathers.

Augustine[70]

Patrick makes no explicit reference to Augustine, nevertheless his theology resonates with the teaching of Augustine. Patrick alludes to twenty-eight works by Augustine.[71] Augustine wrote two of his anti-Pelagian treatises at the request of Hilary of Poitiers and Prosper of Aquitaine in order to help them in their polemics with the Pelagian propagandists in Gaul. The first was entitled, *The Predestination of the Holy Ones*. The second was *The Gift of Perseverance*. Let's see what we can glean from them about Patrick.

'The Lord opened my unbelieving mind' (*C*, 2). This sentence originally comes from Acts 16:14. In Acts Paul is preaching and Lydia is listening attentively to him. We read, 'The Lord opened her heart [*cor*] to pay attention to what Paul was saying.' But Augustine, when copying the sacred text, seems to have written 'understanding' ('*sensum*'), instead of 'heart' ('*cor*'). This was probably due to a lapse of memory on

---

70 For a discussion of Patrick and Augustine in the context of the confessional form of writing, see p. 49.

71 See Conneely, *Letters of Saint Patrick*, p. 243.

his part. Patrick tells us that at the time of his capture he had forsaken God and did not keep his commandments. In Pauline language, he was dead in sin. Then God humbled him by permitting him to be captured and enslaved, but God also showed mercy; as we have just read, 'The Lord opened my unbelieving understanding, so that even at that late hour I should be mindful of my sins and turn with all my heart to the Lord my God.' He bestowed on Patrick the gifts of faith, repentance and conversion. He protected him and consoled him.[72]

It would appear that Patrick had access to these writings and very possibly copied from them. The same error (*'cor'* replaced by *'sensum'*) occurs in his *Confession*. This suggests that Patrick may have had one or even both treatises to hand and was copying from one of them rather than directly from Acts. This invites the conclusion that Patrick had a direct acquaintance with those treatises of Augustine which contain these errors.

'God makes believers and listeners in order that they shall be sons of the living God and coheirs with Christ' (*C*, 4, 59). This takes up the language of the Creeds of the Councils of Nicea (325) and Constantinople (381). It is best read as a proem, or formal introduction to the entire *Confession*, though it could also be described as a *confessio fidei*. Patrick's Creed contains the following words: ' … and His Son Jesus Christ, whom we declare to have been always with the Father; before the beginning of the world, begotten of the Father after the manner of Spirit, inexpressibly, before all beginning … And He poured out the Holy Spirit upon us abundantly … who makes believers and listeners in order that they shall be *sons of God and fellow heirs with Christ.'*

Patrick's creed is analogous in its power and positioning to Augustine's great opening descant in the first five chapters of the *Confessions*:[73]'Great art thou, O Lord, and greatly to be praised.' In Patrick's *Confession* it is balanced by the great Christological Doxology[74] (*C*, 59–60). In both places the same quotation from Romans appears: 'sons

72 See Conneely, *Letters of Saint Patrick,* p. 111, 3(a). Patrick's theology of personal conversion.

73 See Finan in Conneely, *Letters of St Patrick*, p. 133.

74 See Hanson, 'Witness from St Patrick to the Creed of 381' *A.B.*, 101, 1983, pp. 297–299. Also, J. E. L. Oulton, *The Credal Statements of St Patrick as Contained in the Fourth Chapter of His Confession: A Study of their Sources*, Dublin and London, 1940.

of the living God and coheirs with Christ' (Rom 8:16, 17). What is of most importance for us is the fact that Patrick keeps closely to the anti-Pelagian and anti-Arian orthodoxy that he has found above all in the writings of Augustine. The sentence we have quoted is clearly Augustinian in inspiration and directly anti-Pelagian: 'He poured out the Holy Spirit upon us abundantly, as gift, and pledge of immortality, *who makes believers* and listeners in order that they shall be sons of God and coheirs with Christ. Him we confess and adore, One God in the Trinity of the Sacred Name' (*C*, 4). The key words are: '… *who makes believers*'. These same words appear in Augustine's *The Predestination of the Saints*, part 34, and in *The Gift of Perseverance*, part 67. Incontrovertibly, we have here, in these two tracts written by Augustine, for circulation in Gaul, the doctrinal and literary inspiration for the phrase we find in the creed: '(God) *who makes believers* and listeners in order that they shall be sons of God and coheirs with Christ.'

Finan writes, 'We would like to know definitively whether St Patrick was (also) influenced by Augustine's model. Suffice it to say that there are very close parallels, and secondly, it would be surprising if St Patrick could use the word *confessio* so frequently and explicitly without any awareness of the great tradition of the form within which he is writing.' He refers to an article by Peter Dronke, 'On St Patrick's Reading'. Dronke believes that there was not direct dependence. It is unlikely that Patrick had Augustine's work to hand when, by then an old man, he composed his own *Confession*, but he could have read it in his student days. Rather than a text lying by Patrick's elbow, the *Confessions* could have been a pervasive informing influence. Having weighed up what Dronke and others are saying, Finan declines to conclude the existence of direct literary dependence.

Instead of a direct literary dependence, we might argue for an indirect literary dependence: Patrick relied on an intermediary source that in turn relied on Augustine or Patrick absorbed an Augustinian influence from the Christian culture of his time in much the same way that although few Catholics have read the documents of the Second Vatican Council (1962–65), its key ideas have entered their minds and hearts.

Augustinian resonances in Patrick

[A] Patrick (*C*, 17)
'I heard a voice say to me: "Look your ship is ready." It was not nearby, but at a distance of perhaps two hundred miles … Shortly after that I took to flight, left the man with whom I had been for six years, and journeyed by the power of God … and I feared nothing until I reached that ship.'

[A] Augustine (Augustine's *Confessions*, V, 29)
'You knew the cause of my going from one country to another, O Lord … My mother followed me down to the sea. She clasped me tight in her embrace, but I deceived her … I persuaded her to remain that night in a place quite close to our ship … that night I slipped away secretly.'

[B] Patrick (*C*, 23)
'There truly I saw in a vision of the night, a man coming as it were from Ireland with countless letters, and he gave me one of them, and I read the beginning … and I was greatly troubled in heart and I could read no further, and so I awoke.'

[B] Augustine (Augustine's *Confessions*, VIII, 12)
'I heard the voice of a boy or girl chanting over and over again, "Pick it up, read it; pick it up, read it." I snatched it up and in silence read the paragraph on which my eyes first fell … I wanted to read no further, nor did I need to …'

[C] Patrick (*C*, 24–25)
'"He who gave his life for you, He it is who is speaking in you;" and at that I awoke rejoicing. And another time I saw him praying within me, and I was as it were within my body, and I heard one above me praying, that is to say, above my inner man).'

[C] Augustine (Augustine's *Confessions*, VII, 10)
'I entered into my inward soul, guided by you. This I could do because you were my helper. I entered, and with the eye of my soul – such as it was – saw above the same eye of my soul and above my mind the

Immutable Light. It was not the common light, which all flesh can see; nor was it above my mind in the same way as oil is above water, or heaven above earth, but higher, because it made me, and I was below it, because I was made by it.'

[D] Patrick (*C*, 27)
'… something I had done one day, in one hour, in my boyhood, when I was not yet in control of myself. I do not know, God knows, if I was then fifteen years old; and I did not believe in the living God, nor had I believed in him from childhood.'

[D] Augustine (Augustine's *Confessions*, II, 3)
During that sixteenth year of my age, I lived with my parents having holiday from school for a time…the thorn bushes of lust grew rank about my head, and there was no hand to root them out.'

[E] Patrick (*C*, 44)
'… I confess to my Lord, and I do not blush before him, because I am not lying: from the time I came to know him, from my early manhood, the love of God and the fear of him have grown in me, and up till now, by the favour of God, I have kept faith.'

[E] Augustine (Augustine's *Confessions*, IV, 16–31)
'O Lord our God, under the shadow of your wings let us hope – defend us and support us. You will bear us up when we are little and even down to our grey hairs you will carry us. For our stability, when it is in you, is stability indeed, but when it is in ourselves, then all is unstable. Our good lives forever with Thee, our good is You Yourself.'

Cyprian
Cyprian (c. 210–258), bishop of Carthage, converted to Christianity in 246, at the age of thirty-five. Two years later he was designated bishop of Carthage, the capital of Roman North Africa, a city second only to Rome itself in the empire. During his ministry the Church suffered persecution under the Emperors Decius and Valerian. Many people

abandoned the faith at that time. When the storms of persecution subsided many of them sought re-admission to the Church. Ought they to be re-admitted? Some said no, but Cyprian did not agree. Cyprian ruled that they must be received subject to their doing 'exemplary penance', because, 'outside the Church there is no salvation'.[75] Cyprian was insistent on the importance of communion with the See of Rome.[76] 'If anyone deserts the Chair of Peter upon whom the Church was built, does that person think that he or she is in the Church?'[77] Another theme of his teaching was the importance of the unity of the Church, symbolised by the seamless garment of Christ.

Cyprian's teaching extended to prayer. His *Treatise on the Lord's Prayer* is profound. He stresses that the Lord's Prayer is in the plural. 'Our prayer is public and common; and when we pray we pray not for one, but for the whole people, because we the whole people are one.' Pope Benedict XVI says, 'Ultimately, Cyprian placed himself at the root of that fruitful theological and spiritual tradition which sees the heart as the privileged place for prayer.'[78]

We have no evidence other than that of the texts themselves that Patrick read Cyprian. Bieler contends that it is 'beyond doubt' that Patrick 'borrowed' from Cyprian, while Mohrmann disagrees.[79] Conneely and his editors link him to Patrick at five places, one in the *Letters of Cyprian*, and four in his *Treatise on the Lord's Prayer*. Let us look at three passages: two from the *Treatise* and one from letter 67:

(1): '*Non concupisces rem proximi tui. Non occides. Homicida non potest esse cum Christo*' (Cyprian, *Treatise on the Lord's Prayer*, section 24). These words appear verbatim in Patrick's *Letter to Coroticus* (*LC*, 9).

(2): '*nec non in secundis sed etiam in pressuris, ut quidquid mihi evenerit sive bonum sive malum aequaliter debeo suscipere*' (Cyprian, *Treatise*

---

75 Cyprian, *Letters* 4, 4 and 73, 21.

76 Cyprian, *On the Unity of the Church*, 6.

77 Cyprian, *Unity*, 4.

78 Benedict XVI, *The Fathers of the Church*, London: CTS, 2008. At title: 'He who gave us life, also taught us how to pray.'

79 Bieler, 'The Place of St Patrick in Latin Language and Literature', p. 69. Mohrmann disagrees with Bieler's reading, see *Four Lectures*, pp. 7–8.

on the Lord's Prayer, section 27). These words appear verbatim in Patrick's *Confession*, 'You who helped my work with such Divine Power that today among the nations I steadfastly exalt and glorify your name wherever I am; and that, *not only when circumstances favour me but also where I am afflicted*; so that whatever happen to me, I must accept with an even mind, and give thanks to God who showed me that I should believe him' (*C*, 34).

(3): '*Quis sanctorum non horreat iocundare vel convivium fruere cum talibus*' (Cyprian, *Letters of Cyprian*, 'Letter 67'). These words appear verbatim in the *Letter to Coroticus* (*LC*, 13).

Hilary

Hilary of Poitiers (c. 310–c. 367) was born into a wealthy though non-Christian family. After a long quest for the truth about God, humanity and life, he was baptised about the year 345 and ten years later elected bishop of Poitiers. Banished to Phrygia (Turkey) by the Emperor under pressure from the pro-Arian bishops of the south of Gaul (modern-day France), he devoted his time to his next major work, a dogmatic *Treatise on the Trinity* developing his entire Trinitarian theology on the liturgical formula of Baptism: *In the name of the Father and of the Son and of the Holy Spirit.*

Patrick's work shows frequent linkage with Hilary's *Treatise on the Psalms* and *On the Trinity*. Hilary would devote the rest of his life to defending faith in the divinity of Jesus Christ as defined by the Council of Nicaea. In these years he also composed a *Commentary on the Gospel of Matthew*, the earliest extant commentary in Latin.

Hilary's banishment to the East occasioned his encounter with the Creed of Nicea. As Conneely notes, Hilary's banishment emphasises the influence of the Greek-speaking East on the West, especially with regard to matters of heresy and the unity of Church.

Patrick in his time

The textual connections between Patrick and the Fathers are disputed by scholars. The reception of Patrick, however, is not just a matter for scholars. Patrick's writings have a theological and pastoral significance, especially to the Irish Church. It is important that Patrick is understood in the context of his own time, not as an outlier but as a missionary called by God. The context provided by the Fathers, especially in regard their experiences of exile and martyrdom (both red and white) and their struggles against heresy (both Arian and Pelagian), is important for understanding Patrick. As Conneely writes in the *Letters of Saint Patrick* (p. 186), 'assessing the Christian and theological content of the fifth-century pastorals of St Patrick has a historical dimension which is specifically patristic . . . a spiritual grasp of the substance of the Gospel and of faith in it, [and] a historical sense of the Age of the Fathers of the Church and of patristic theology – these are all important for any theological appraisal of St Patrick's writings.'

5: Patrick's Spiritual Legacy

'When you search for me, you will find me; if you seek me with all your heart' (Jer 29:13)

We will start this review of Patrick's spiritual doctrine[80] with a consideration of his experience as a slave in Ireland. Slavery and liberation by divine intervention were the foundational experiences of Patrick's Christian discipleship. While he was in Ireland, Patrick tells us, he searched for God earnestly, and there he found Him. He encountered God by means of prayer and searching. 'After I came to Ireland, I was daily herding flocks, and I used to pray many times a day, and the love of God and the fear of Him came to me, and my faith increased' (*C*, 16). The God whom he encountered, who let himself be found, was the God and Father of Our Lord Jesus Christ, the Father of Mercies. 'God,' says Patrick, 'opened my unbelieving mind, … so that I should remember my sins and turn with all my heart to the Lord my God, who looked upon my abjection, and had mercy on my youth and ignorance, and watched over me before I knew him … and he kept me safe and comforted me as a father would his son' (*C*, 2).

Patrick's faith life was marked by a deep attachment to God the Father. Patrick, an old man now, reflecting on his past life, finds that his heart is overflowing with gratitude to the God who has given him so much (*C*, 38), consoling and comforting him so often in his sorrows, beginning from the time of his enslavement until his final liberation (*C*, 17). Compare this with what God says to Moses at the burning bush, 'I have observed the misery of my people who are in Egypt; I have heard

---

80 By this expression I mean the themes of his teaching which one would expect the saint to stress and dwell on.

their cry on account of their taskmasters. Indeed, I know their suffer ings, and I have come down to deliver them from the Egyptians' (Ex 3:7–8). Since then Patrick knew him as a most dear Father, 'infinitely loving, protective and merciful' (*C*, 2).

Flowing from love of the Father was a deep love for Christ. In *Confession* 13 it was this devotion to Christ that motivated him. If we look at *Confession* 24, when Satan harassed him, we see that Patrick believed that he was aided by 'Christ my Lord and His Spirit'. He himself is 'a letter of Christ' (*C*, 11) bearing salvation to the uttermost parts of the earth. He is an ambassador for Christ (*C*, 56; *LC*, 5). Furthermore, he knows that he will be judged by Christ (*C*, 8).

As a bishop he is committed to upholding the dogmatic teaching of the Council of Nicea concerning Christ. Patrick's *confessio fidei* (*C*, 4) contains the contains the anti-Arian formula, 'His Son Jesus Christ whom we declare to have always been with the Father.' Note also the solemn doxology at *Confession* 60: 'We are a people who believe in the true Sun and adore Him, Christ, who will never perish … no one who does the will of Christ will ever perish: but he will abide forever, as Christ abides forever, He who with God the Almighty Father and with the Holy Spirit reigns before all ages, as now, and forever, and ever. Amen.'

Patrick gradually lets himself be led more and more by the Holy Spirit, who is 'the gift of God', 'the power from on high' whose presence he has experienced with special intimacy in prayer and dynamic action in his daily life. If we look for evidence, *Confession* 40 provides it in abundance. The entire chapter is devoted to the Spirit and mission, including a long quotation from the prophet Joel, which is read at Mass on Pentecost Sunday. The reader has only to look at the rich series of allusions (*C*, 20, 25, 33, 43, 46). 'The Spirit makes believers in order that they shall be sons and daughters of God and co-heirs with Christ.'

Patrick's teaching of the Trinitarian Mystery is experientially supported by the action of the Three Divine Persons in his life as related in the *Confession* and celebrated in this doxology. The humble shamrock calls us to faith in God the Father, in his only begotten Son Jesus Christ, and in the Holy Spirit who proceeds from the Father and the

Son, and together with them is adored and glorified.

God's gift to Patrick

Two other major themes of Patrick's spiritual doctrine should be mentioned. They are, firstly, thanksgiving for the 'Gift of God', which Patrick must make known to all people, and secondly the saint's sense of 'indebtedness to God' (*C*, 38). 'What return shall I make?'

We have seen that the phrase 'Gift of God' occurs several times in the *Confession*. Patrick says: 'It is my duty to make known the Gift of God and his everlasting consolation' (*C*, 14); 'I must not hide the Gift of God which he bestowed on me in the land of my captivity' (*C*, 33); 'If I have accomplished anything the credit is not due to me, it was all the Gift of God' (*C*, 62).

'What was the source of that Gift, so great, so salutary, of knowing and loving God even to the point where I should forsake my homeland and family?' (*C*, 36). The question is of course rhetorical. God himself is the source, like the merciful Father in Luke's Gospel, rich in mercy, patient and full of love (Lk 15:11–31). Patrick also asks in words taken from Psalm 116:12, 'What shall I return to the Lord for all his bounty to me?' His answer is, 'by exalting and praising His wonderful deeds before every nation under the whole heaven' (*C*, 3).

The expression 'gift of God' is found in John's Gospel (Jn 4:10). In John 'living water' (flowing water) is normally understood to mean 'the Holy Spirit'. In *Confession* 14, Patrick speaks of 'the "gift of God" and His everlasting consolation'. Both expressions are used in John's Gospel and are taken as referring to the Holy Spirit. Indeed the title 'paraclete', which Jesus applies to the Holy Spirit, means 'one urgently called upon to give counsel and help in a struggle, a Consoler'(Jn 14:15–17; 16:13–15). Patrick also speaks of 'that gift, so great, so salutary' that he has received and which is, he explains, that of knowing God and also loving him (not without suffering and loss freely accepted). The gift of knowing and loving God can only be bestowed by God, through the action of the Spirit of God. Hence, Paul tells us that when we were baptised the gift of the love of God was poured into our hearts by the Holy Spirit which was given to us (Rom 5:5).

The expression 'gift of God', a gift which, Patrick is convinced 'must be made known to all', puts us in mind of another phrase to be found in Romans, 'the mystery kept secret for endless ages' (Rom 16:25, 26).[81] For Paul 'the mystery kept secret for endless ages' is God's saving design centred on Christ. It is the totality of the divine plan, now revealed in the Church and made known to all the nations. In Colossians he asks for prayers that he may be given a good opportunity to preach Christ's message, 'to tell the secret of Christ'. 'Pray that I may preach in such a way as to make it clear, as I should' (Col 4:3). Patrick believes that he has a similar duty to make known the gift of God which he has received, and in fact he has dedicated his whole adult life to that mission.

The task of making the gift of God known to all people rests on Patrick's shoulders, identical with his missionary vocation, and on those who have faith in Jesus Christ (*C*, 14). It is a duty, but it is also a joy and a privilege. His stress on 'gift' has perhaps as background the anti-Pelagian insistence on grace as the free gift of God. God gives grace freely. Theology and the Sacred Liturgy speak frequently of the 'grace of the Holy Spirit'. In the Sacrament of Anointing of the Sick the sacramental words begin as follows, 'By this holy anointing may the Lord in his love and mercy help you with the grace of the Holy Spirit … '. In the great hymn for Pentecost, *Veni Creator Spiritus*, the Holy Spirit is invoked under the title 'gift of God' *(donum Dei)*. The term 'gift of God' then refers to the Holy Spirit personally, at work in the hearts of those who welcome him and allow themselves to be guided by him. In the case of Patrick it refers to his whole life of discipleship, in particular his missionary vocation, which bore abundant fruit for God's kingdom.

Patrick has received 'that Gift, so great and so salutary, of finding God and knowing and also loving Him'. He must make this wonderful experience known to others in order that they too may share in it. He writes, 'I take this to be a measure of my faith in the Trinity that, without regard to danger, I should make known the gift of God' (*C*, 14). He says that he must not hide the Gift of God; he believes that God has preserved him from all iniquities through his in-dwelling Spirit who

---

81 Romans 16:25, 26. See Bieler (ed.), *The Patrician Texts in the Book of Armagh,* Dublin Institute for Advanced Studies, 1952. 'The expression *donum Dei* is used of the Holy Spirit, of God as "giver of comfort."'

has worked 'to this day' within him (*C*, 33).

He ends his *Confession* with these words, 'If I have ever accomplished or brought to light any small part of God's purpose, none shall ever assert that the credit is due to my own self, but regard it rather as a true fact to be firmly believed, that it was all the "Gift of God". And that is my confession before I die' (*C*, 62). Since his conversion Patrick has been a servant of God's design, and he knows that God has blessed his efforts at serving him.

Patrick's use of Scripture

It is no surprise to learn that Patrick quotes most often from the Psalms.[82] Next in order of preference are quotations from Romans, then Acts, followed by Matthew and both letters to the Corinthians. There are numerous quotations from the other Gospels, Prophets and Wisdom Literature, even the Book of Tobit. In all, Patrick refers to fifty-four of the books that go to make up the Bible. 'This is extraordinary, given that his correspondence is only two pastoral letters.'[83]

Some scholars have suggested that Patrick's frequent quotations of Scripture were a strategy for overcoming the deficiencies in his command of Latin by making use of more Scripture than might normally be expected, but I doubt this. Patrick uses Scripture because it is inspired by the Holy Spirit and is the Word of God, a Word ever actual.

With reference to Matthew, Raymond E. Brown says, 'Although modern scholars generally begin their Gospel studies with Mark, the oldest of the written gospels, Matthew stood first in most ancient biblical witnesses and has been the Church's Gospel *par excellence*. Indeed, the Gospel according to Matthew has served as the foundational document of the Church, rooting it in the teaching of Jesus; a Church built on rock against which the gates of hell would not prevail. Matthew's Sermon on the Mount, the eight Beatitudes, and the Lord's Prayer are among the most widely known treasures in the Christian heritage. Organizational skill and clarity, plus a penchant for unforgettable images,

---

82 For the data given in this part I am drawing on Bieler, 'Der Bibeltext des Heiligen St Patrick' in Biblica 28, 1947, pp. 31–58, 236–263.

83 Conneely, *Letters of Saint Patrick*, p. 161.

have given this Gospel priority as the Church's teaching instrument.'[84]

As we have already observed, in the early centuries of the Church's history Matthew was highly valued for catechetical and preaching purposes. Patrick makes more use of it than of any other Gospel. It is no surprise then to find that at *Confession* 40 he inserts two important missionary quotations from Matthew: 'This gospel of the kingdom will be preached throughout the whole world ... and then the end will come' (Mt 24:14); 'Go, therefore, make disciples of all nations, baptising them in the name of the Father, and of the Son, and of the Holy Spirit ... '(Mt 28:19). The third quotation is taken from Mark. 'Go therefore into all the world, preach the Gospel to every creature' (Mk 16:15). Patrick also quotes Hosea, 'Those who were not my people I will call my people' (Hos 2:25).

This is where Patrick found the missionary mandate of the Church and his personal vocation. From the time of his conversion until his death Patrick worked as a missionary, convinced that God had called him personally to carry out this work. For Patrick his missionary vocation was a task, 'It is our duty to fish well and diligently' (*C*, 40), but it was also a sacred gift for which he would be ever grateful to God.

Patrick and Ireland

It is no surprise that when Patrick thinks of God he almost always thinks of the Irish nation and prays for them. 'May my God preserve me from ever losing His people, the people He has won for himself in the furthest parts of the earth' (*C*, 58). Patrick loves the Irish as a father loves his children. He is committed to their welfare despite having been kidnapped and enslaved at their hands. He cannot bear the thought that they should ever fall away from Christ. We underline the theme of Patrick's spiritual fatherhood of the Irish people. He speaks of his heavy workload, 'my toil-filled ministry as a bishop' (1 Cor 9:16). He is like Paul, who never can forget that it was he who evangelised the Corinthians and therefore became their father in the Lord, 'For though you might have ten thousand guardians in Christ, you do not have many

---

84   R. E. Brown, *Christ in the Gospels of the Ordinary Sundays*, Collegeville, MN: The Liturgical Press, 1998.

fathers. Indeed, in Christ Jesus I fathered you through the gospel' (1 Cor 4:15).

A unique feature of the mission to Ireland is that it was directed to a people who had never been conquered by Rome and as a result had never been romanised. The Irish were categorised as barbarians, people who had a poor grasp of Latin, and were regarded as inferior. Patrick is aware of this. 'They are disdainful towards us because we are Irish' (*LC*, 16). In effect, Patrick, who previously was a proud Roman patrician, is now content to number himself with the Irish. He has like Paul become all things to all men in order to save at least some of them.

Jesus says in the Gospel, 'And this good news of the kingdom will be proclaimed throughout the world, as a testimony to all the nations' (Mt 24:14). The evangelisation of Ireland is representative of this. We read, 'We are the witnesses that the Gospel has been preached to the limit beyond which no one dwells' (*C*, 34).

Patrick sees a direct relationship between the preaching of the Gospel 'to the uttermost parts of the earth' (meaning Ireland), and the end of human history (C, 38–39). Once the Gospel had been preached 'to the ends of the earth' there would be no further reason to delay the *parousia* (the second coming of Christ and the end of the world).[85] Patrick may have expected that the *parousia* would be soon. He may even have expected it during his lifetime. His mission to Ireland may have had an eschatological character for him. After all, the Gospels are full of parables in which we are exhorted to make ready. We are counselled in the Gospels and the letters of Paul to prepare for it and pray for its coming: *Maranatha. Come, Lord Jesus.*

Patrick has received a powerful insight into the mystery of God's loving, protective and merciful fatherhood, and at the same time he is deeply conscious of his own spiritual fatherhood of the Irish nation. Other people, entire nations, are invited to experience God's generous love. This too is the 'gift of God' and it must be made known.

---

85 Thomas O'Loughlin, *Saint Patrick: The Man and His Works*, London: Triangle, 1999, p. 44.

6: Patrick, Father of the Church?

We have seen the most important themes of Patrick's spiritual doctrine. Patrick clearly has much to teach us. This is a good moment to ask whether or not he himself should be recognised as a Father of the Church. The most obvious objection that can be raised against this proposal is that his writings are insufficient in quantity to enable the reader to form an opinion on a particular point. Placed in comparison with the writings of Augustine or Ambrose, Patrick's work appears slight indeed. This ought not to disqualify him. Jesus himself never wrote anything, except on one famous occasion when he scraped some words in the sand (Jn 8:6). Socrates, the Greek philosopher, never wrote anything either. Furthermore, what Patrick did write, though brief, is very profound and reflects the experience of an exceptionally wise and holy man who loved God and put himself at God's service wholeheartedly.

There is plenty of evidence that Patrick was a gifted and committed missionary bishop and an effective preacher and teacher. 'I am very much indebted to God', Patrick says, 'who granted me so great a grace that through me a multitudinous people should be reborn for God and afterwards confirmed; they who never had knowledge of God, but up until now worshipped only idols and abominations, have lately been made "a people of the Lord," and are called "children of God."'

Patrick wrote two documents that, though short, reveal a profundity of thought and spiritual insight that make him worthy to be compared with the great saints. As well as that, he was a man of deep prayer. He tells us in his *Confession* that as a slave in Ireland he began to pray up to a hundred times in the day and the same number of times during the night, and that he continued the practice throughout his captivity. In this way he grew in familiarity with God.

As we have seen, Patrick's prayer was Trinitarian, starting from the first Divine Person, the Father of Mercies, moving on to reverent and loving dialogue with the Incarnate Word, Christ, whom he adored as *Sol verus* (the true sun – this in a country whose inhabitants were sun worshippers) or *Sol justitiae* (sun of justice). Lastly he prayed to the Holy Spirit who comes to help us in our weakness, and whose help we, like Patrick, should ask for continuously.

Patrick makes no reference to Our Lady, but it must be remembered that the Council of Ephesus that defined Mary as *Theotókos*, Mother of God, did not take place until 431 (coincidentally, the same year as that of the mission of Bishop Palladius to Ireland).

Noel Dermot O'Donoghue stresses that Patrick must be taken seriously as the privileged recipient of many mystical experiences and as a teacher of prayer, passing on to others what he has experienced personally – *contemplata aliis tradere*. His mystical experiences , apparitions, locutions, etc., are evidence of divine favour.

Bishop William Philbin, in the preface to his book, *Mise Pádraig* (his translation into Irish of the *Confession* and *Letter to Coroticus*) draws attention to the visible, world-wide devotion to Patrick. 'There are more churches', he says, 'dedicated to St Patrick than to any other saint, with the exception of Our Lady, and perhaps, St James the Apostle'. Despite this global significance it can be suggested that one of the reasons why Patrick is not thought of as a Father of the Church has to do with the perception of Ireland being geographically remote.

Patrick was a man who could deal with kings and prelates confidently. The skills involved were employed by him 'for the sake of the Gospel and for no other motive'. Even when dismissed from his office he displayed great resilience and was finally reinstated.

As we have seen, orthodoxy was of great importance to the Fathers. Any person who exercises a teaching role must take care to teach sound doctrine. They must correctly grasp Catholic teaching, think with the Church, and let themselves be guided by the Sacred Magisterium. When comparing Patrick with the Fathers, we must ask 'Was he orthodox?' The anti-Pelagian and anti-Arian strands in Patrick's writings make it clear that like the Fathers he was orthodox. As a missionary to Ireland his teaching was sound, and he resisted the heresies of his time.

Conclusion

And now my hand is weary, like the hand of the scribe. We have arrived at point, where, I believe, I can conclude. What can we say about St Patrick? Surely, we must say of him that he is truly one of the very great saints. The effort we make to have an insight into his mind and heart is amply repaid. We have seen that the writings of Patrick provide abundant evidence of contact with the Latin Fathers. We have also studied Patrick's spiritual doctrine and have concluded that there is a strong case for including Patrick among the Fathers of the Church.

In closing, we can fittingly compare Patrick to Paul, whom he admired so much. Like Paul, Patrick, though of noble blood made himself a servant of men, 'To the weak I became weak, to win over the weak. I have become all things to all men, to save at least some. All this I do for the sake of the Gospel, so that I too may have a share in it' (1 Cor 9:19). He felt called to evangelise like Paul, 'Woe to me if I do not preach the Gospel' (1 Cor 9:16). In making the gift of God known to the Irish he himself became a gift to them, a gift which, God willing, this nation will always treasure.

Appendix 1:
Letter to Coroticus

1 I Patrick, a sinner and unlearned, resident in Ireland, declare myself to be a bishop. I believe with complete certainty that it is from God I received what I am. I dwell, then, among non-Roman people, a stranger and exile for the love of God; He is my witness that it is so. Not that I wished anything so harsh and so rough to come from my lips; but I am driven by zeal for God, and the truth of Christ has provoked me, for love of the neighbours and sons for whom I have given up homeland and family, and my life even unto death – should I be worthy of that. I live for my God, to teach the heathens, even if I am despised by some.

2 With my own hand I have composed and written these words, to be given, sent and delivered to the soldiers of Coroticus; I do not say, to my fellow citizens, or to fellow citizens of the holy Romans, but to fellow citizens of the demons because of their evil deeds. In enemy fashion they live in death, allies of the Scotti and the apostate Picts. Bloodstained men bloodied in the blood of innocent Christians, whom I have begotten in countless numbers unto God, and have confirmed in Christ!

3 The day following that on which the white-robed neophytes had been anointed with chrism – it was still fragrant on their foreheads when they were cruelly butchered and put to the sword by those I have named – I sent a letter with a holy priest whom I had taught from his infancy, clerics accompanying him, to ask that they give us back some of the booty and of the baptized captives they had taken. They made a mockery of the messengers.

4 Hence I know not for which I should grieve the more; whether for those who have been slain, or those taken captive, or those whom the devil has grievously ensnared. Together with him they will be the slaves of hell in everlasting punishment, because he who commits sin is indeed a slave, and is called a son of the devil.

5 Consequently let every God fearing person know that they are excommunicate from me, and from Christ my God for whom I am an ambassador. Parricides! Fratricides! Ravenous wolves gobbling up the people of the Lord like bread on the table! As Scripture says: *Lord, the wicked have destroyed your law,* which in these the last times He had successfully and graciously planted in Ireland, and which had grown up by the favour of the Lord.

6 I am no maker of false claims. I have a share with those whom he called and predestined to preach the Gospel amid no small persecutions unto the farthest part of the earth, even if the enemy gives vent to his malice through the tyranny of Coroticus, who has no reverence for God or for His bishops, whom He chose, and to whom He granted the highest, divine, sublime power, that those whom they should bind on earth would be bound also in Heaven. This, then, you holy and humble of heart, is my most earnest plea to you: It is not lawful to pay court to such people, or to eat or drink with them; nor may their alms be accepted, until, through rigorous penance, unto the shedding of tears, they render satisfaction to God, and free the menservants of God and the baptized maidservants of Christ, for whom He died and was crucified.

7 The Most High rejects the gifts of the wicked. The man who offers a sacrifice from the property of the poor is like one who slays a son in sacrifice before his father's eyes. *The riches,* says Scripture, *which he gathered unjustly shall be vomited up from his belly; the angel of death drags him away; with the fury of dragons he shall be beaten; the viper's tongue shall slay him; unquenchable fire shall devour him.* Therefore: *Woe to those who fill themselves with what is not their*

own. And again: *What does it profit a man that he should gain the whole world and suffer the loss of his own soul.*

8 It would be tedious to examine every single text, or even to indicate them – to gather from the entire range of the Law the testimonies concerning such greed. Avarice is a deadly sin. *You shall not covet your neighbour's goods. You shall not kill.* A murderer cannot be with Christ. He who hates his brother is accounted a murderer. Or: *He who does not love his brother remains in death.* How much more is he guilty who has stained his hands with the blood of children of God, whom he recently acquired for Himself in the uttermost parts of the earth through the Gospel message from my own lowly person!

9 Was it without the inspiration of God, or on my own merely human initiative, that I came to Ireland? Who drove me to it? It is by the Spirit I am bound, to the extent of no longer seeing anyone of my own kindred. Is it from myself there springs the holy mercy I exercise towards that people who once took me captive and carried off the menservants and maidservants of my father's house? I am freeborn by descent: I am the son of a *decurion.* The fact is that for the benefit of others I sold my freeborn state – I am not ashamed of it, and I have no regrets; in short, I am a slave in Christ to a foreign people for the sake of the inexpressible glory of the eternal life which is in Christ Jesus our Lord.

10 And if my own know me not, [it is true that] *a prophet has no honour in his own country.* Could it be that we are not from one sheepfold, and do not have one God for our Father? As Scripture says: *He who is not with me is against me, and he who does not gather with me scatters.* Is it not well said that *one man pulls down and another builds up?* I seek not my own interest. It was not I but God's grace that put this anxious concern into my heart, to be one of the hunters and fishers whom long ago God foretold He would send in the last days.

11 I am looked on with malice. What am I to do, Lord? I am greatly despised. Behold, your sheep are butchered and ravaged around me, by all that band of robbers under orders from the evil-minded Coroticus. Far from the love of God is he who betrays Christians into the hands of Scotti and Picts. Ravenous wolves have gobbled up the flock of the Lord, which in Ireland under excellent care was really flourishing – [so well that] the sons of the Scotti and the daughters of their kings who have become monks and virgins of Christ are beyond my power to number. Take no pleasure then in the wrong done to the just; even unto hell it shall be unacceptable.

12 Which of the saints would not shrink in horror from making merry with such persons, or enjoying a banquet in their company? They have filled their houses with the spoils of dead Christians; they live on plunder. They know not, the wretches, that they are offering deadly poison as food to their friends and children, as Eve did not understand that it was really death she was handing to her husband. Such are all who do evil: they wreak death as their eternal punishment.

13 The following is the custom of the Christians of Roman Gaul: they send chosen and holy men to the Franks and other heathen peoples with so many thousands of *solidi* to ransom baptized captives. But your way is to slay them, or sell them to a foreign nation that knows not God; you hand over the members of Christ as it were to a brothel. What sort of hope have you in God, you or anybody who approves of you, or communes with you in words of flattery? God will judge. For it is written: Not only they who do evil, but also they who approve of them, shall be condemned.

14 I know not what more I can say, or express, concerning the departed ones of the children of God whom the sword has stricken with such dire cruelty. For it is written: *Weep with those who weep;* and again; *If one member suffers, let all members suffer with*

it. The Church therefore wails and weeps for those of her sons and daughters not yet slain by the sword, but deported and exported to distant lands; where grave sin openly and shamelessly abounds, there freeborn men and women have been put up for sale, Christians have been reduced to slavery – and worst of all, slavery to vile, depraved, apostate Picts.

15 Therefore in sadness and grief I shall cry out: O my fairest and fondest brothers and sons, whom beyond numbering I have begotten in Christ, what shall I do for you? I am not fit to come to the aid of God or of men. The wickedness of the wicked has prevailed over us. We are turned as it were into foreigners. Maybe they do not believe that we have received one and the same baptism, or that we have one and the same God as Father? For them it is a matter of disdain that we be Irish. As Scripture says: Have you not one God? Why have you abandoned each one of you his neighbour?

16 Therefore I grieve for you, I grieve, my dearest ones. But then again, I rejoice within myself. I have not laboured for nothing, nor has my exile been in vain. This crime so horrendous, so unspeakable, has indeed been perpetrated, but thanks be to God, my baptized believers, you have gone from this world to paradise. I can see you: you have begun your migration to where there shall not be night any more, nor mourning, nor death; but you shall skip for joy like calves loosed from their bonds, and you shall tread down the wicked, and they shall be ashes under your feet.

17 You, therefore, shall reign with the apostles and the prophets and the martyrs. You shall take possession of everlasting kingdoms, as Christ himself testifies when he says: They shall come from the east and from the west and sit at table with Abraham and Isaac and Jacob in the kingdom of heaven. Outside shall be the dogs and the sorcerers and the murderers; and: As for liars and perjurers, their lot shall be in the lake of everlasting fire. Not

without cause does the apostle say: Seeing that the righteous man shall only with trouble be saved, the sinner then and the impious transgressor of the law – where will he find himself?

18 Coroticus then and his miscreants, rebels against Christ, where shall they discover their place to be, sharers out of young Christian women as booty for the sake of a wretched temporal kingdom which will pass away in a moment of time? As a cloud or smoke that is scattered by the wind, so shall deceitful sinners perish at the presence of the Lord; but the just, strong and unchanging, shall banquet with Christ; they shall judge nations, and rule over wicked kings forever and ever. Amen.

19 I testify before God and His angels that all shall be as He has made it known to my own unlearned self. It is not my words that I have set forth in Latin, but the words of God, and of His apostles and prophets, who have never lied. He who believes shall be saved, but he who does not believe shall be condemned – it is God who has spoken. I request with the greatest gravity – whatever servant of God agrees to be the bearer of this letter – that it be on no account withdrawn or hidden from anybody, but rather be read before all the communities, even in the presence of Coroticus himself. But if God inspires them to return, at some time or another, to a right mind towards God, so that even at a late hour they repent of such an impious deed – murder of the brethren of the Lord – and so release the baptized women captives they previously seized; if God thus inspires them, so that they deserve to live unto God and be made whole here and in eternity, peace be to them with the Father and the Son and the Holy Spirit. Amen.

Appendix 2:
Confession

1. I am Patrick, a sinner, unlettered, the least of all the faithful, and held in contempt by a great many people. I am the son of Calpornius, a deacon, son of Potitus, a priest. My father lived at the village of Bannavem Taburniae, for he had an estate nearby, where I was taken captive at about sixteen years old. I did not know the true God, and for this reason I was led in captivity to Ireland, with so many thousands of people. It was in accordance with our deserts, because we had forsaken God and did not keep His commandments, and were not obedient to our bishops who used to admonish us for our salvation. God brought to bear upon us the wrath of His anger and scattered us among many peoples, even to the uttermost part of the earth, where now, in my lowliness, I dwell among strangers.

2. And there the Lord opened my unbelieving mind, so that even at that late hour I should remember my sins and turn with all my heart to the Lord my God, who looked upon my abjection, and had mercy on my youth and ignorance, and watched over me before I knew Him, and before I came to be wise, or to discern between good and evil; and He kept me safe and comforted me as a father would his son.

3. And that, then is why I cannot remain silent, nor is it expedient that I should, about such great favours and so great a grace as the Lord deigned to bestow on me in the land of my captivity. Because this is the return we can make after God corrects us and brings us to know Him: to exalt and praise His wonderful deeds before every

nation under the whole heaven.

4. Because there is no other God, nor was there ever before, nor will there be hereafter, except God the Father, unbegotten, without beginning, from whom is all beginning, containing all things, as we have been taught; and His Son Jesus Christ, whom we declare to have been always with the Father; before the beginning of the world begotten of the Father after the manner of Spirit, inexpressibly, before all beginning; and through Him were made all things visible and invisible. He was made man, and having conquered death He was received in heaven into the presence of the Father. And He gave Him all power above every name in heaven, on earth, and under the earth; and let every tongue confess to Him that Jesus Christ is Lord and God, in whom we believe in and whose coming we look for soon, to be judge of the living and the dead, and to render to every one according to his deeds. And He poured out the Holy Spirit upon us abundantly, as gift, and pledge of immortality, who makes believers and listeners in order that they shall be sons of God and fellow heirs with Christ. Him we confess and adore. One God in the Trinity of the Sacred Name.

5. For the Lord himself said through the prophet: *Call upon me in the day of your trouble; and I will deliver you, and you shall glorify me.* And again He says: *It is honourable to reveal and confess the works of God.*

6. Notwithstanding that I am in many things imperfect I want my brethren and kinsmen to know what sort of man I am, so that they may be able to perceive the desire of my soul.

7. I am not ignorant of the testimony of my Lord, who declares in the Psalm: *You will destroy those who speak falsely.* He says again: *A lying mouth destroys the soul.* And the same Lord says in the Gospel: *On the day of judgement men will render account for every careless word they utter.*

8. I have every ground, then, in fear and trembling to dread this sentence on that day when no-one shall be able to withdraw or hide himself, but when we shall all, without exception, render account of even the smallest sins before the judgement seat of Christ the Lord.

9. For those reasons I long ago thought of writing, but I have hesitated until now for fear of what critics should say. Because I was not a student as others were, who thus thoroughly drank in the law and the holy Scriptures, the two in equal measure, and never changed their language from childhood but rather were always engaged in perfecting it. Whereas I have had to change my language and speak that of a foreign people, as may easily be proved from the flavour of my writing, which shows how poorly I am instructed and how little skilled in expressing myself. As Scripture says: *Through the way he expresses himself shall the wise man be discerned, and his understanding, and knowledge and instruction in truth.*

10. But what will an excuse avail me (even when it is in accordance with the truth), especially when the excuse is accompanied by presumption? Here am I in my old age seeking something I did not acquire when I was young: my sins prevented me from mastering what I had read through in only a perfunctory way. But who will believe me even if I repeat what I have said? As an adolescent, indeed as almost a speechless boy, I was taken captive before I knew what I should seek and what I should avoid. And so today I am ashamed and greatly afraid to expose my ignorance, because to people trained in self-expression I am unable to express myself briefly, as my spirit and mind long to do, in such a manner that what I say will reveal my feelings.

11. But if what was given to others had been given to me I certainly would not have remained silent, because of my duty to return thanks, as I was saying; and if, perhaps, in doing so now I may appear to some to be pushing myself forward with my lack of

knowledge and my difficulty in expressing myself, Scripture also says: *The tongues of stammerers will quickly learn to speak peace.* How much more ought we seek to speak who are, says Scripture, *a letter of Christ bearing salvation to the uttermost parts of the earth;* and, if not an elegantly written letter, yet a letter firmly and powerfully written on your hearts, not with ink, but with the Spirit of the living God. And the Spirit further testifies: *Even rusticity was created by the Most High.*

12. Wherefore although I was at first an unlettered exile, truly ignorant, who knew not how to provide for the life hereafter, I know this for a certainty: that assuredly before I was humbled I was like a stone lying in deep mire; and that He who is mighty came and in His mercy lifted me up; and, more than that, truly raised me aloft and placed me on top of the wall. It is therefore my bounden duty to cry out aloud in order to make some return to the Lord for such great favours of His here and in eternity, favours which it is beyond the mind of man to measure.

13. Wherefore, wonder you at this, you great and small who fear God; and you, lordly and clever men of letters, listen, and examine closely what I am about to say. Who was it that roused me, a fool, from the midst of those who are wise, and learned in the law, and skilled in speaking and in general affairs; and in preference to others inspired me, me whom this world rejected, to be such a man, (if only I were!), as in awe and reverence and without cause of complaint would faithfully work for the good of the people to whom the love of Christ brought me and made a gift of me for the duration of my life (if I should be worthy of it); to be, in a word, a man who would humbly and sincerely serve them to the end?

14. In proportion, then to the faith which I have received from the Trinity, it is my duty to make this choice: without thought of the risk of censure I incur, to make known the gift of God and

His everlasting consolation; fearlessly and confidently to spread God's Name everywhere; so that even after my death I may leave a legacy to my brethren and sons whom I have baptized in the Lord – so many thousands of people.

15. And I was not worthy, nor such a sort that the Lord should grant this to His little servant; that after my so numerous hardships and troubles, after my captivity, after many years had gone by, He should bestow on me so great a grace in favour of that people – a thing that once, in my youth, I never expected nor thought of.

16. But after I came to Ireland I was daily herding flocks – I used to pray many times a day – more and more the love of God and the fear of Him came to me, and my faith was increased, and my spirit was moved so that in one day I would pray as many as a hundred times, and in the night nearly as often, even while I was staying in the woods and on the mountain; and before daylight I used to be stirred to prayer, in snow, in frost, in rain; and I felt no ill effects from it, not was there any sluggishness in me, such as now I see there is, because then the spirit was fervent in me.

17. And there, as it happens, one night in my sleep I heard a voice say to me: 'It is good that you fast, you who are soon to go to your own country'. And after a little while again I heard a voice say to me: 'Look, your ship is ready'. It was not nearby, but was at a distance of perhaps two hundred miles; and I had never been there, nor did I know anybody there. Shortly after that I took to flight, left the man with whom I had been for six years, and journeyed by the power of God, who directed my way unto my good, and I feared nothing until I reached that ship.

18. And on the day I arrived the ship left its anchorage and I spoke to the crew that I might have the possibility of sailing with them, but the captain was displeased and answered sharply in anger: 'On no account are you to try to go with us' and when I heard

that I withdrew from them to go to the little hut where I was staying, and on the way I began to pray, and before I had finished my prayer I heard one of them who was shouting loudly after me: 'Come quickly, for these people are calling you'; and immediately I went back to them and they began to say to me: 'Come, for we take you on trust; make friends with us in any way you wish'; and that day, accordingly, I refused to suck their breasts through fear of God, but rather hoped that some of them would come to faith in Jesus Christ, for they were heathens; and thus I had my way with them, and straight away we set sail.

19. And after three days we reached land, and for twenty-eight days we journeyed through deserted country, and food failed them and hunger overcame them, and one day the captain said to me: 'How now, Christian? You say your God is great and all-powerful; why then can't you pray for us? For we are in danger of starving; it will go hard with us ever to see a human being again'. I said confidently to them: 'Turn sincerely with all your heart to the Lord my God, because nothing is impossible to Him, so that today He may send you food in your way until you are satisfied, because He has abundance everywhere'. And with the help of God it so came to pass: lo, a herd of pigs appeared on the way before our eyes, and they slaughtered many of them, and their bodies were refreshed, for many of them had collapsed and had been left half dead by the wayside. And after this they gave full thanks to God, and I became honourable in their eyes; and from that day they had food in abundance; they even came upon wild honey, and they offered me a share of it, and one of them said; 'It is a sacrificial offering'. Thanks be to God, I tasted none of it.

20. That very same night I was sleeping when Satan mightily put me to the test – I shall remember it as long as I am in this body. He fell upon me like a huge rock, and I could not move a limb. But whence did it occur to me, ignorant in spirit, to call upon Helias? And while this was happening I saw the sun rise in the heavens,

and as I was crying out: 'Helias, Helias', with all my strength, lo the splendour of that sun fell on me and promptly shook all heaviness from me; and I believe that I was aided by Christ my Lord, and that His Spirit was even then crying out on my behalf; and I hope that it will be so in the day of my distress, as He says in the Gospel: *In that day,* the Lord testifies, *it is not you who speak, but the Spirit of your Father speaking through you.*

21. And again, many years later, I was once more taken captive. When I was with them, accordingly, for that first night I heard a divine voice telling me: 'For two months you will be with them'. And that was what actually came to pass: on the sixtieth night the Lord delivered me from their hands.

22. Even on the journey He provided us daily with food and fire and dry quarters, until on the tenth day we reached human habitation. As I related above, for twenty-eight days we journeyed through deserted country, and on that night in which we reached human beings we had, in fact, no food left.

23. And once more, after a few years I was in Britain with my family, who received me as a son, and sincerely begged of me that at least now, after all the many troubles I had endured I should not leave them to go anywhere. And there, truly, I saw in a vision of the night, a man coming as it were from Ireland, whose name was Victoricus, with countless letters, and he gave me one of them, and I read the beginning of the letter, which ran: 'The Voice of the Irish'; and as I was reading the beginning of the letter aloud I thought I heard at that very moment the voice of those who lived beside the wood of Voclut, which is near the Western sea, and thus they cried out as with one voice: 'We beg you, holy youth, to come and walk once more among us'. And I was greatly troubled in heart and could read no further, and so I awoke. Thanks be to God that after many years the Lord granted them according to their cry.

24. And on another night – I do not know, God knows, whether it was in myself or beside myself – very distinctly in words which I heard but could not understand except at the end of the prayer, He thus declared Himself: 'He who gave His life for you, He it is who is speaking in you'; and at that I awoke rejoicing.

25. And another time I saw Him praying within me, and I was as it were within my body, and I heard [One] above me, that is to say above my inner man; and there He was praying earnestly, with sighs; and as this was happening I was in amazement and wonder and puzzlement about who it was that was praying within me. But at the end of the prayer He declared that He was the Spirit; and at that I awoke, and I recalled what the apostle had said: *The Spirit helps the weaknesses of our prayer; for we do not know how to pray as we ought; but the Spirit himself pleads for us with sighs unutterable that cannot be put into words.* And again: *The Lord our Advocate pleads for us.*

26. And when I was tested by some of my seniors, who came and cast up my sins as unfitting me for my laborious episcopate, assuredly on that day I was sorely tried, to the point where I could have fallen here and forever; but the Lord graciously spared the alien and stranger for His Names' sake; and He came powerfully to my aid when I was being walked upon, so that I did not fall unhappily into discredit and disgrace. I pray God that it be not accounted to them as a sin.

27. They found occasion for their charge against me – after thirty years – in a deed I had confessed before I became a deacon. In my anxiety I confided to my best friend, my mind full of sorrow, what I had done one day in my boyhood, indeed in one hour, because I was not yet in control of myself. I know not, God knows, if I was then fifteen years old; and I did not believe in the living God, nor had I believed in Him from childhood, but remained in death and unbelief until I was severely chastised and

truly humbled by hunger and nakedness – and that, daily.

28. In contrast, I was not setting out for Ireland until I was approaching my declining years, but this was in fact to my advantage, for in the interval I was corrected by the Lord, and so fitted by Him that today I should be what once was far beyond me: that I should be concerned or active myself about the salvation of others, at a time when I was taking no thought even for myself.

29. And so, on the day when I was rejected by the above mentioned persons – that night I saw a vision in the night, I looked [and] before my face was a writing that stripped me of my honour. And as I looked at it I heard a divine voice say to me: 'We have seen with disapproval the face of so-and-so' (designated by name). Nor did He say: '*You* have seen with disapproval', but: '*We* have seen with disapproval'. As if He had associated Himself with me. As He said in Scripture: *He who touches you is as one who touches the apple of my eye.*

30. This is why I give thanks to Him who in all things gave me strength, so that He did not hinder me from the journey I had decided on, nor from the work of mine which I had learned from Christ my Lord, but rather did I feel in myself no little power from Him, and my fidelity was approved before God and men.

31. Wherefore I say boldly that my conscience does not reproach me now, and will not hereafter: I have God as my witness that I have not lied in the words I have reported to you.

32. Rather do I grieve for my best friend, that he should have given cause for our hearing such a statement from the Lord. A man to whom I had entrusted my very soul! And I had learned from some of the brethren before that gathering at which my defence came up – I was not present at it, nor was I in Britain, nor did the matter originate from me – that he too would argue for me

in my absence; even to myself he had said with his own mouth: 'Look, you must be raised to the episcopate' – of which I was not worthy. But why did it occur to him afterwards that before everybody, good and bad, he should put me even publicly to shame [for a deed] for which he had earlier freely and gladly granted me pardon – as did the Lord, who is greater than all?"

33. I have said enough. I must not, however, hide the gift of God which He bestowed on me in the land of my captivity, because then I earnestly sought Him and there I found Him, and He preserved me from all iniquities (so I believe) through His indwelling Spirit, who has worked to this day within me. I am speaking boldly again. But God knows that if a mere man had declared this to me I should perhaps have remained silent, for the love of Christ.

34. Wherefore I give unwearying thanks to my God, who kept me faithful in the day of my trial, in such ways that today I may confidently offer Him my life in sacrifice, as a living victim to Christ my Lord. [I give unwearying thanks to my God] who delivered me from all my troubles, so that I can even say: 'Who am I, Lord, or what is my calling?' – You who helped my work with such divine power that today among the nations I steadfastly exalt and glorify Your Name wherever I am; and that, not only when circumstances favour me, but also when I am afflicted; so that whatever happens to me, good or bad, I must accept with an even mind, and thank God always; God showed me that I should believe Him endlessly to be trusted; and who so helped me that I, a man ignorant [of His designs], in the last days should dare to undertake this work so holy and so wonderful; in such fashion that I might in some degree imitate those whom the Lord already long ago foretold would announce His Gospel in witness to all nations before the world's end. And as we have seen it written, so we have seen it fulfilled: behold, we are the witnesses that the Gospel has been preached to the limit beyond which no-one dwells.

35. It would take too long to relate all my labours, one by one or even in part. Briefly let me say how the most gracious God often freed me from slavery, and from the twelve perils in which my life was at stake, in addition to many plots against me, and things I cannot express in words. Nor shall I bore my readers. But I have God as my witness, who knows all things even before they come to pass, how a divine voice often forewarned me, poor ignorant ward that I was.

36. Whence was this wisdom given to me, who had it not of myself, I who knew not the number of my days nor had any mind for God? Whence was I afterwards granted that gift so great, so salutary, to know God and also to love Him, even to the point where I should forsake my homeland and my family?

37. And many gifts were offered to me with weeping and tears, and I gave offence to the givers; and not [to them only, but also], against my wish, to some of my seniors. But under God's guidance, in no way did I consent or give in to them. It was not I but the grace of God, who overcame in me and resisted all those things, so that I came to the heathen Irish to preach the Gospel and to endure insults from unbelievers; to hear myself taunted for being a foreigner; [to experience] many persecutions unto bonds; and to surrender my free-born status for the benefit of others. And if I shall be found worthy of it, I am ready to give even my life unhesitatingly and very gladly for His Name's sake; and there I desire to spend it until I die, if the Lord will grant me that.

38. Because I am exceedingly in debt to God, who granted me so great a grace that through me a multitudinous people should be reborn in God, and afterwards confirmed; and that clerics should everywhere be ordained for them – for a people newly coming to belief whom the Lord took from the uttermost parts of the earth, as long ago He had promised through His prophets: To you the nations will come from the uttermost parts of the earth

and say, Our fathers got for themselves worthless idols, and there is no profit in them. And again: I have set you to be a light for the Gentiles, that you may bring salvation to the uttermost parts of the earth.

39. And there I wish to await His promise, who certainly never deceives, as He promises in the Gospel: They will come from east and west and sit at table with Abraham and Isaac and Jacob, just as we believe that from the whole world believers shall come.

40. For that reason, accordingly, it is indeed our duty to fish well and diligently, as the Lord fore-admonishes and teaches, saying: Follow me, and I will make you fishers of men. And again He says through the prophets: Behold, I am sending fishers and many hunters, says God; and so on. We were gravely bound, then, to spread our nets, so that a great multitude and throng should be caught for God, and that everywhere there should be clergy to baptise and exhort a needy and thirsting people, as the Lord in the Gospel admonishes and teaches, saying: Go therefore now, make disciples of all nations, baptizing them in the name of the Father and of the Son and of the Holy Spirit, teaching them to observe all that I have commanded you; and lo, I am with you always, to the close of the age. And again He says: Go therefore into all the world and preach the Gospel to the whole creation. He who believes and is baptized will be saved; but he who does not believe will be condemned. And again: This Gospel of the kingdom will be preached throughout the whole world, as a testimony to all nations; and then the end will come. And again the Lord announces beforehand through the prophet; And in the last days it shall be, God declares, that I will pour out my Spirit upon all flesh and your sons and your daughters shall prophesy, and your young men shall see visions, and your old men shall dream dreams; yea, and on my menservants and my maidservants in those days I will pour out my spirit; and they shall prophesy. And in Hosea He says: Those were not my people I will call 'my

people' and her who had not received mercy I will call 'her who has received mercy'. And in the very place where it was said, 'You are not my people', they will be called 'sons of the living God'.

41. Consequently, in Ireland, they who never had knowledge of God, but up until now always worshipped only idols and abominations – how they have lately been made a people of the Lord and are called children of God; sons of the Scotti and daughters of their kings are seen to be monks and virgins of Christ!

42. And there was even one blessed Scottic girl of noble birth, very beautiful, full-grown, whom I baptized; she came to us a few days afterwards for one reason only: to tell us she had received a message from a messenger of God who instructed her to become a virgin of Christ and to draw close to God. Thanks be to God, six days later she most laudably and ardently laid hold of that life. [For] what all the virgins [do] they [the Irish] likewise do; not with their parents' consent, rather do they suffer both persecutions and false reproaches from their families; and nevertheless, their number ever increases [in fact from those of our own race born there we do not know the number who have become virgins of Christ], not counting the widows, and the married persons who practise continence. But among them slave girls are in greatest trouble; they suffer continually, even to the extent of terror and threats. But the Lord has given grace to many of His handmaids, because even though they are forbidden they continue steadfast in their following of Him.

43. As a result, then, even if I should wish to leave them and make a journey to Britain – and I would most dearly love to make that journey, so as to see my homeland and family; not only that, but also [to proceed] as far as Gaul to visit the brethren and see the face of the saints of my Lord: God knows I greatly desired it – still I am bound by the Spirit, who testifies to me that if I do this He will pronounce me guilty; and I am afraid of losing the labour I

began, and not I but Christ the Lord, who ordered me to come and be with those people for the rest of my life – if God wills it, and keeps me from every evil way, so that I sin not in His sight.

44. This, indeed, it is my duty to hope for, but my own self I do not trust as long as I am in this body of death. For he is strong who daily strives to subvert me from fidelity, and from the chastity I have undertaken, in devotion unfeigned to Christ my Lord, to the end of my life. But the hostile flesh is always pulling us towards death, that is to say, towards the unlawful satisfying of what it entices us to do. And I know this in part because I have not always led a perfect life, as other believers have. But I confess to my Lord, and do not blush before Him, because I am not lying: from the time I came to know Him, from my early manhood, the love of God and the fear of Him have grown in me, and up till now, by the favour of the Lord, I have kept faith.

45. Let who will laugh and scorn: I shall not be silent, nor do I hide the signs and wonders which were shown to me by the Lord many years before they came to pass, by Him who knows all things even before the beginning of time.

46. That is why, then, it is my duty to give unceasing thanks to God, who often pardoned my lack of wisdom and my negligence; and who on more than one occasion held back from vehement anger with me, who had been chosen as His helper and yet was slow to act in accordance with what I had been shown and what the Spirit was prompting me. And the Lord had mercy on me thousands of times because I saw in myself that I was ready, but that I did not know how to direct myself in regard to the matter, for many were trying to forbid this mission of mine; among themselves they were even talking behind my back, and asking: 'What is that fellow thrusting himself into danger among a hostile people who do not know God?' They said this not out of malice, but because it did not make sense to them, for the reason that, as I myself bear

witness, I was uneducated. And I myself was slow to recognize the grace that was then in me; now I understand – what I ought to have understood earlier.

47. Now, then, I have given an honest account to my brethren and fellow servants, who have believed me because of what I have proclaimed and am proclaiming, in order to strengthen and confirm your faith. My desire is that you also strive after greater things, and do more excellent deeds. This will be my glory, because a wise son is the glory of his father.

48. You know, and God knows, how I have lived among you from my early years, in true faith and in sincerity of heart. Even in respect to those heathens among whom I dwell, I have kept my word with them, and will continue to keep it. God knows I have deceived none of them, nor do I have any intention of doing it, for the sake of God and of His Church, lest I should stir up persecution for them and for us all, and lest the Name of the Lord should be blasphemed through me; for it is written: Woe to the man through whom the name of the Lord is blasphemed.

49. For although I am very inexperienced, I have nevertheless tried in some measure to keep my reserve even from the Christian brethren and the virgins of Christ and the religious women who used to make me little gifts spontaneously, and would cast something from their ornaments on to the altar. These I would return to them, and they would be annoyed with me for doing so. But I [did it] for the hope of eternal life: that for the sake of it I should in all things act with circumspection, in such a way that they should not accept me or the ministry of my service on any ground that did not pertain to the Faith; and so that I should give no opportunity to unbelievers, even in the least matter, to defame or disparage [me].

50. But when I baptized so many thousands of people, did I perhaps

look for even half a screpall from any of them? Give me the evidence, and I will restore it to you. Or when the Lord ordained clerics everywhere through my insignificant person, and I shared the ministry with them for nothing, if I demanded from any of them so much as the price of even my shoe, testify against me and I shall restore it to you.

51. On the contrary, I paid out monies for your sake, that they might accept me; and I journeyed among you, and everywhere, in your interest, in many dangers, even to the remotest parts beyond which nobody lived, and whither no-one had ever come to baptize, or ordain clerics, or confirm the people; by gift of the Lord I did it all, with diligence and great joy, for the sake of your salvation.

52. And all that time I used to give presents to the kings, in addition to paying wages to their sons who travel with me; and nonetheless they seized me with my companions, and on that day they were keen and avid to kill me, but my time had not yet come; and everything they found with us they seized, and myself they bound in irons; and on the fourteenth day the Lord freed me from their power; and all our belongings were also restored to us, for the sake of God and the close friends with whom we had provided ourselves beforehand.

53. But you know yourselves how much I paid out to those who wielded authority throughout the districts I more frequently visited. For I estimate that I distributed to them not less than the price of fifteen men, so that you might have the benefit of my presence, and I might always have the joy of your presence before God. I do not regret it, not do I count it enough: I am still spending, and will spend more; for the Lord has the power to give me the privilege later of being spent myself for your souls.

54. Behold, I call God to witness upon my soul that I am not lying:

and it is not to provide an occasion for your flattering me or ministering to my greed, that I have written to you. Nor is it that I am looking for honour from any of you. Enough for me that honour which is as yet not seen but which is believed in with the heart; He who has promised is faithful; He never lies.

55. But even in this present world I see myself exalted beyond measure by the Lord. And I was not worthy of it, nor was I of the sort that He should bestow it on me; for I know as a certainty that poverty and adversity are better suited to me than lucre and luxury. But Christ the Lord, too, was poor for our sake. And I poor and needy as I am, even if I were to wish for wealth, I no longer have it; nor can I judge what my future is going to be; because daily I expect to be slaughtered, or defrauded, or reduced to slavery, or to any condition that time and surprise may bring. But I fear none of these things because of the promise of Heaven, for I have cast myself into the hands of Almighty God, who rules everywhere. As the prophet says: Cast your care upon God, and He will sustain you.

56. Behold, then, I now commend my soul to my most faithful God, for whom I am an ambassador in my lowliness. But He is no accepter of persons, and for this office He chose me from among His least ones, that I should be one of His ministers.

57. Let me make return to the Lord then for all His bounty to me. But what shall I say, or what shall I promise to my Lord? – for I am unable to do anything unless He himself enables me. But let Him search my heart and my mind, for with desire I desire, and ready I would be, to drink of His chalice, as He granted it to many others who loved Him.

58. Wherefore may my God preserve me from ever losing His people, the people He has won for Himself in the furthest parts of earth. I pray God that He may give me perseverance, and deign to keep

me a faithful witness to Him until I die, for the sake of my God.

59. And if in my life I have ever achieved any good for the cause of my God whom I love, I ask Him to let me shed my blood with those who are exiles and captives for His name, even if I should go without burial itself, or should my wretched remains be divided, limb by limb, among dogs or wild beasts, or should birds of the air devour them. I hold it as certain, that if this should happen to me, I shall have gained my soul along with my body, because without any doubt we shall rise on that day in the glory of the Sun: that is to say, in the glory of Christ Jesus our Redeemer, as sons of the living God and fellow heirs with Christ and destined to be conformed to His image: because it is from Him, and through Him, and in Him that we are to reign.

60. For that sun which we see [with our bodily eyes] rises daily at God's command for our sake; but it will never reign, nor will its splendour abide; but all who adore it will come, as unhappy men, unhappily to punishment. We, on the other hand, [are a people] who believe in the true Sun and adore Him, Christ, who will never perish. And neither will he who does His will; but he will abide for ever, as Christ abides for ever, He who with God the Almighty Father and with the Holy Spirit reigns before all ages, as now, and for ever and ever. Amen.

61. Here then, one more time, let me briefly set down the theme of my confession, I testify in the Truth, and in exultation of heart before God and His holy angels, that I never had any reason other than the Gospel and its promises for ever returning to that race from whom, in an earlier time, I had barely made good my escape from captivity.

62. And now, to all who believe and hold God in reverence, should one of them condescend to inspect and accept this writing put together in Ireland by Patrick, a mere unlettered sinner, this is my

prayer: that if I have accomplished or brought to light any small part of God's purpose, none shall ever assert that the credit is due to my own uneducated self, but regard it rather as a true fact to be firmly believed that it was all the gift of God. And that is my confession before I die.

Further Reading

On Patrick

Conneely, D., *The Letters of Saint Patrick*, Maynooth: An Sagart, 1993.

De Paor, Máire B., *Patrick the Pilgrim Apostle of Ireland*, Dublin: Veritas, 1998.

Duffy, J., *Patrick in His Own Words*, Dublin: Veritas, 2000.

Hanson, R .P. C., *The Life and Writings of the Historical Saint Patrick*, New York: Seabury Press, 1983.

Howlett, D., *The Book of the Letters of Saint Patrick the Bishop*, Dublin: Four Courts, 1994.

Losak, M., *Rediscovering St Patrick: A New Theory of His Origins*, Dublin: Columba Press, 2016.

Mohrmann, C., *The Latin of Saint Patrick: Four Lectures*, Dublin, DIAS, 2009.

On Medieval Ireland

Charles-Edwards, T. M., *Early Christian Ireland*, Cambridge: CUP, 2014.

Ó Cróinín, D., *Early Medieval Ireland: 400–1200*, Abingdon: Routledge, 1995.

Kenney, J., *The Sources for the Early History of Ireland: Ecclesiastical – An Introduction and Guide*, Dublin: Four Courts Press, 1993.

Richter, M., *Medieval Ireland*, Dublin: Gill and Macmillan, 2005

Walsh, J. and Bradley, T., *A History of the Irish Church 400–700 AD*, Dublin: Columba Press, 1991,

The Fathers
Athanasius, *Life of Anthony*
Augustine, *Confessions*
– *Soliloquies*
Cyprian, *Letters*
– *Treatise 4: On the Lord's Prayer*
Hilary, *On the Trinity*
– *Treatise on the Psalms*
Ignatius, 'Letter to the Romans'
Jerome, *Letters*
Justin, *Dialogue with Trypho*
– *First Apology*

On the Fathers
Hamman, A., *How to Read the Church Fathers*, London: SCM Press, 1993.
O'Meara, J., *The Young Augustine: An Introduction to the Confessions of St Augustine*, Harlow: Longman, 1980.

A Note on Fr Daniel Conneely and Fr Patrick Bastable

Fr Daniel Conneely SSC
Fr Conneely was the editor of *The Far East* magazine and spiritual director of students in St Columban's College, Navan, Co. Meath in 1961, at the time when he made his discovery concerning Patrick's knowledge of the Fathers of the Church.

Fr Patrick Bastable SSC
Fr Bastable taught philosophy at St Columban's, Dalgan Park, University College Dublin and St Patrick's College, Maynooth. He was general editor of Fr Conneely's papers after his death and edited his book, *The Letters of St Patrick*, for publication.